Table of Contents

Introduction 1

Chapter 1: The Parish 7
- Pastors and Evolving Models of Parish 12
- Service to Parish and Community 15
- Service to National and Global Communities 21
- Recognition of Limitations 23
- Empowerment of Lay Leadership 24

Chapter 2: Catechesis in the Parish 29
- What Is Catechesis? 34
- Important Goals in the Life and Mission of the Parish 37
- Ministry of the Word 41
- The Woven Fabric of Catechesis 43
- Adult Directed Catechesis 47
- Family as Primary Catechist 50

Chapter 3: The Priest in Catechetical Ministry 59
- The Role of the Priest in Catechetical Ministry 66
- Realistic Appraisals 71
- Time Allocation for Catechesis 75
- Being Present to People 78
- Pervasiveness of Catechesis 79
- A Balanced Approach 81

Chapter 4: The Priest as Empowerer of Catechetical Ministry 89
- How Priests Empower 98
- Roleplay Scenarios and Guidelines 102
- Roleplay 1 – Responsibility for the Catechetical Program .. 105
- Roleplay 2 – Parental Involvement in Sacramental Programs . 111
- Roleplay 3 – Potential Catechist 119
- "What Made Me the Priest I Am Today?" 125
- Catechetical Actions 127

Chapter 5: Conclusions 135
- Empowerment Insights to Share 137
  - Catechists 137
  - Catechetical Leaders 138
  - Priests 139
  - Bishops 140
- Questions and Challenges 142
- Conclusion and Summary Points 150

Chapter 6: Creating Action Plans 155

Chapter 7: The Symposium Process 167

Appendix 1: The Symposium Participants 179

Appendix 2: Documents in this Book 181

Appendix 3: Selected Bibliography 183

Dedication

This book is dedicated to the priests who attended the symposium
in grateful recognition of their forthrightness
in sharing their insights and experiences,
and with sincere thanks for all they have done
in their service to the Church.

The Priest as Empowerer of Catechetical Ministry

Report and Workbook
based on the
Symposium
The Priest as Empowerer of the Catechist

Symposium Designers and Facilitators
Dr. Gerard F. Baumbach
James J. DeBoy, Jr.

Symposium Project Writer
William M. Ippolito

Symposium Book Advisory Group
Dr. Eleanor Ann Brownell
Helen Hemmer, IHM
Rev. Terry M. Odien
Neil A. Parent
Karen Ryan

NATIONAL CONFERENCE OF
CATECHETICAL LEADERSHIP
Washington, DC

William H. Sadlier, Inc.

New York, NY

Copyright © 1995 by William H. Sadlier, Inc.
All rights reserved. This book, or any part
thereof, may not be reproduced in any form,
or by any means, including electronic,
photographic, or mechanical, or by any sound
recording system, or by any device for the
storage or retrieval of information, without
the written permission of the publisher.
Printed in the United States of America.

Credits appear on page 188.

Home Office:
9 Pine Street
New York, NY 10005-1002

ISBN: 0-8215-9950-X

1 2 3 4 5 6 7 8 9 / 9 8 7 6 5

Introduction

As members of the living Christ, incorporated into him and made like him by baptism, confirmation and the Eucharist, all the faithful have an obligation to collaborate in the expansion and spread of his Body, so that they might bring it to fullness as soon as possible.
Decree on the Church's Missionary Activity, 36

Jesus calls all members of the Church to "make disciples of all nations" (Matthew 28:19). The responsibility for conversion has always included the entire Church community, and the documents of the Second Vatican Council and those that followed have increasingly reinforced this point. Yet today many Catholics still perceive evangelization as the work of missionaries among people who are not Catholic in foreign lands or at home.

Evangelization is ever present and embraces the entire spectrum of faith—from helping to enrich those who live and practice the Catholic faith to helping bring the invitation of God's message to those who exist entirely without a belief in God. Pope Paul VI, in his Apostolic Exhortation *On Evangelization in the Modern World*, states that evangelization "is a complex process made up of varied elements: the renewal of humanity, witness, explicit proclamation, inner adherence, entry into the community, acceptance of signs, apostolic initiative. These elements may appear to be contradictory, indeed mutually exclusive. In fact they are complementary and mutually enriching. Each one must always be seen in relationship with the others." (*Evangelii Nuntiandi*, 24)

Pope John Paul II affirms in *Catechesi Tradendae* that catechesis is one of these elements, "a very remarkable one—in the whole process of evangelization." (*Catechesi Tradendae*, 18) And explaining that Christ is "at the heart of catechesis," the *Catechism of the Catholic Church* states: "From this loving knowledge of Christ springs the desire to proclaim him, to 'evangelize,' and to lead others to the 'yes' of faith in Jesus Christ. But at the same time the need to know this faith better makes itself felt." (*Catechism of the Catholic Church*, 429)

Late in 1992 the National Conference of Catholic Bishops approved a national plan for evangelization in the United States. Published in February 1993, *Go and Make Disciples* outlines a detailed strategy for evangelization, calling the Church in the United States "to bring about in all Catholics such an enthusiasm for their faith that, in living their faith in Jesus, they freely share it with others." (*Go and Make Disciples*, page 7)

As *Go and Make Disciples* was being published, twenty-three priests from across the United States participated in "The Priest as Empowerer of the Catechist" symposium which was jointly sponsored by the National Conference of Catechetical Leadership (NCCL) and William H. Sadlier, Inc. Though these two events occurred independently, the insights and experiences shared by the priests during the symposium illustrate how catechetical ministry supports evangelization.

NOTES

Introduction

NOTES

The Symposium

"The Priest as Empowerer of the Catechist" symposium took place from January 31 to February 3, 1993 at Our Lady of Florida Spiritual Center in North Palm Beach, Florida. The symposium was conceived as a way to explore approaches to catechetical ministry with priests who are recognized for their work with and through catechists. The participants are priests who help to build faith communities whose members have the strength and commitment to spread the word of God.

In his welcoming remarks, William Sadlier Dinger, president of Sadlier, explained that the symposium was conceived as a way to gather and explore with priests "this important (catechetical) work of the Church and to discover concrete ways to share, help and support parish priests and catechists across the country." Specifically, the symposium had a twofold objective:

- To identify elements needed for parish priests to empower those who serve in catechetical ministry;
- To identify concrete ways of helping and supporting parish priests in their empowering ministry.

To accomplish these objectives, the symposium was designed as an interactive process of shared dialogue. There was no position paper drafted ahead of time to be used as a focus for discussion. Catechetical professionals at the symposium did not suggest to the group of assembled priests what they should be doing in the area of catechetical ministry. Instead, the symposium proceeded with the view that the assembled priests themselves were the experts. Before the symposium, each participant was asked to prepare responses to reflection questions based on the four topics which functioned as the informational structure of the symposium. The responses served as the basis for the examination of each of these areas:

- The Parish
- Catechesis in the Parish
- The Priest in Catechetical Ministry
- The Priest as Empowerer of Catechetical Ministry

The process used a variety of creative techniques to facilitate discussion in order to focus on what the priests presently do in parish life and in catechetical ministry. James J. DeBoy, Jr., President of NCCL at the time of the symposium and Director of Religious Education for the Archdiocese of Baltimore, and Dr. Gerard F. Baumbach, Vice President and Publisher of Sadlier, designed the process and facilitated the proceedings. Both have many years of catechetical experience on a wide variety of levels.

Though the pastoral plan *Go and Make Disciples* was not part of the symposium discussions, the participants' approach to building the Church reflects the recommendations of the document. The topic of the symposium focused on catechesis and the empowerment of catechists and catechetical ministry, and the discussions revealed how catechesis and evangelization are in a synergistic relationship in the ministry of the participants.

The participants' approach to catechesis also reflects the teaching of *Sharing the Light of Faith: National Catechetical Directory for Catholics of the United States* (*NCD*): "To consider evangelization only as a verbal proclamation of the gospel robs it of much of its richness; just as it does not do justice to catechesis to think of it as instruction alone. Like evangelization, catechesis is incomplete if it does not take into account the constant interplay between gospel teaching and human experience—individual and social, personal and institutional, sacred and secular." (*NCD*, 35)

The Participants

In order to assemble a suitable cross section of pastoral experience, NCCL Provincial Representatives nominated priests whom they believed could bring "the excitement and the vision to the theme of the symposium." From these nominations came twenty-three priests from diverse regions of the nation. Representatives from the National Conference of Catechetical Leadership, William H. Sadlier, Inc., and the National Catholic Educational Association also participated.

Most of the priests were pastors. However, their experience, age, and background varied significantly. The assembled priests were ordained from four to thirty-four years. The parish situations represented by the group were diverse—from inner city to rural mission, from wealthy suburb to farming community. Some came from parishes with several people on staff, while others were much more limited in size. The size of the parishes varied from 3,000 to 300 families. Twelve of the pastors headed parishes with Catholic schools, with one also responsible for a parish high school.

Coming from such diverse backgrounds, the participants naturally approached topics from different perspectives. But throughout the symposium there was a genuine respect for who they were and what they were trying to accomplish. There was no hesitation to be frank with the group. During the symposium the participants delighted in the successes of others and were not hesitant to speak about their own efforts that may have fallen short.

The participants affirmed the faith and dedication of catechists, Directors of Religious Education, and other catechetical leaders without distinguishing whether by vocation they were lay or religious. The participants did, however, give witness to the tremendous contributions the faithful have made and continue to make in catechetical ministry throughout the nation.

Through the ensuing discussions it became evident that the assembled priests possessed a vision of the church rooted in the Second Vatican Council. It also became clear that empowering catechists and catechetical ministry is symptomatic of their approach to building the Church. The symposium was indeed fortunate to benefit from the willing and open participation of these priests.

Introduction

NOTES

Using this Book: Entering the Discussion

"But grace was given to each of us according to the measure of Christ's gift. . . . And he gave some as apostles, others as prophets, others as evangelists, others as pastors and teachers, to equip the holy ones for the work of ministry, for building up the body of Christ . . . ."

Ephesians 4: 7, 11–12

One clear benefit of the symposium was its focus on what the gathered priests are *presently* doing in catechetical ministry. This emphasis enabled the participants to draw from their pastoral experience and to examine directly their parishes' current, positive, and enriching catechetical undertakings. The process can help you do the same. The book builds upon the symposium and the wisdom that it surfaced, but it is more than a summary report or a set of conclusions. It is a means that you can use to review your parish's catechetical ministry using the experiences of the symposium's participants as a point of comparison.

Throughout this book, you are invited to complete the same activities and answer the same questions as the symposium's participants. Place yourself in the discussion, reacting and reflecting on what is said. If you have a response, if a thought comes to you, record it in the "Notes" column next to the paragraph. The process can help you clarify areas that may be vague, identify areas that may be absent, and highlight areas that may be strong. You may also choose to engage others in discussion as you explore these questions.

Prior to the symposium the participants received a booklet of reflection questions and were requested to respond as best they could before the symposium so that the event could begin with a "reservoir of response." This enabled the facilitators and participants to build on concrete experience as they worked to identify ways that priests empower catechists and catechetical ministry.

These questions served to focus the direction of the symposium, and they provide the same role in this book. The questions are grouped according to the four segments of the symposium process, which in turn are covered as chapters of this book. Some questions may pique your interest or reflect your experience more than others. However, your discernment process will benefit if you answer all the questions as completely as possible. As you do this, also draw upon the insights of others who work with you in catechetical ministry. The process for reflection and response remains the same for each of the chapters.

Suggestions for Using this Book

As you review the catechetical experiences of the priests who attended the symposium, and also consider your own catechetical experience, there are suggested steps that you can follow.

- First, answer the reflection questions.

- Second, read the summary of the corresponding symposium discussion. Responses from the completed booklets submitted by the participants are incorporated into this summary, and they also appear intermittently on the bordered pages throughout the chapters. Since the booklets were designed as an aid for the participants, not everyone submitted a copy of these responses. In addition, one person who was unable to attend the symposium itself completed and submitted a booklet. His thoughts are also incorporated in this material.

- Third, reflection questions, based on the symposium discussions, appear throughout the chapter to help you identify and record your initial reactions and thoughts.

- Fourth, after reading the chapter, use the symposium discussions as a benchmark for comparison as you revisit your responses to the reflection questions at the beginning of the chapter. You may find that you overlooked some things, or underestimated the impact of others.

- Fifth, after considering the symposium discussions, your reflections, and your responses to the questions, you may want to identify some initial areas for further consideration. Are there ideas or activities that you would like to incorporate into your parish program? Are there current activities in your parish that you would like to reinforce? A worksheet at the end of each chapter provides space for you to record your thoughts.

- Finally, a planning section appears in Chapter 6. Here you and others can create action plans based on the information gathered during this process.

The chapters contain references to catechetical documents, documents of the Second Vatican Council, and other teaching documents of the Church that are pertinent to the topic. These are identified by the document title and section number in parentheses following the citation. For example: (*Catechesi Tradendae*, 18). When a document does not contain paragraph numbers, the page is cited. If you are unfamiliar with a source, Appendix 2 provides brief descriptions of the documents quoted in this text. The Selected Bibliography in Appendix 3 offers the bibliographic information for these sources.

Finally, in addition to the clergy, many others can benefit from this examination of ways in which priests empower catechetical ministry. Parish Directors of Religious Education, Principals, catechists, teachers, youth ministers, and parish catechumenal teams will also find the report, questions, and commentary to be a valuable resource for their varied ministries.

Prayer

Prayer was an integral aspect of the symposium experience. A prayer service marked the beginning and the end of each day, and the symposium concluded with a eucharistic liturgy. As you proceed through this book, whether you are reading this on your own or are completing this process with others, you are encouraged to approach the material and the exercises in a prayerful manner. Be open to the insights of the Holy Spirit. If you are working through this material with others, please spend time together in prayer as part of this process.

Introduction

NOTES

Reflection

As you begin this process, take some time to reflect on the prayer offered by Pope John Paul II at the conclusion of the Apostolic Constitution, *Fidei Depositum*, the document presenting the *Catechism of the Catholic Church*.

I beseech the Blessed Virgin Mary, Mother of the Incarnate Word and Mother of the Church, to support with her powerful intercession the catechetical work of the entire Church on every level, at this time when she is called to a new effort of evangelization. May the light of the true faith free humanity from the ignorance and slavery of sin in order to lead it to the only freedom worthy of the name (cf. Jn. 8:32): that of life in Jesus Christ under the guidance of the Holy Spirit, here below and in the Kingdom of heaven, in the fullness of the blessed vision of God face to face (cf. 1 Cor 13:12; 2 Cor 5:6–8)!

Catechism of the Catholic Church, page 6

Chapter 1
The Parish

NOTES

Introduction

The parish is not principally a structure, a territory or a building, but rather, "the family of God, a fellowship afire with a unifying spirit," (Lumen Gentium, 28) "a familial and welcoming home," (Catechesi Tradendae, 67) the "community of the faithful." (Canon 515.1) Plainly and simply, the parish is founded on a theological reality, because it is a Eucharistic community.

Christifideles Laici, 26

Ministry does not take place in a vacuum, and neither does the leadership style of a pastor. Therefore, an examination of ways in which a priest empowers catechists and catechetical ministry begins with an overview of the parish. As one of the participants observed: "We tend to underestimate the impact a parish has. The parish is a support community in faith to many people and it provides many opportunities of faith growth."

From the moment of baptism, an individual becomes a member of a new and larger family who together share the life of Christ—the Christian community. The parish provides the locus for this community, offering activities that spiritually nourish the members so, as a group and individually, they can grow in faith. This growth is nurtured by catechesis, which "aims therefore at developing understanding of the mystery of Christ in the light of God's word, so that the whole of a person's humanity is impregnated by that word." (*Catechesi Tradendae*, 20)

The parish helps facilitate the four dimensions of catechesis: message, community, worship, and service. The message revealed by God, *kerygma*, is proclaimed by the Church. Catechesis is part of community in the life of the Holy Spirit, *koinonia*. It leads to and flows from the ministry of worship, *leiturgia*, which sanctifies through prayer and sacrament. And catechesis supports the ministry of service to the Christian community and the entire human community, *diakonia*. This results in efforts to achieve social justice and has traditionally been expressed in spiritual and corporal works of mercy. (cf. *NCD* 32, 213)

Personal spiritual growth is part of a larger commitment. As the *Decree on the Apostolate of Lay People* explains, a person who is baptized becomes part of the apostolate committed "to spread the kingdom of Christ over all the earth for the glory of God." (*Apostolicam Actuositatem*, 2) This document later states that "the parish offers an outstanding example of community apostolate, for it gathers into a unity all the human diversities that are found there and inserts them into the universality of the Church." (*Apostolicam Actuositatem*, 10)

However, the catechetical and evangelical mission of the church on the parish level often differs from the parishioners' perception of that mission. A participant offered this observation about his parish. He explained that all the parishioners are at a different place on their faith journey. It appears that approximately thirty percent of the parishioners are deeply involved in the

NOTES

parish and believe the parish is an important part of their lives as individuals and families. These people look to the parish for stability, for assistance in raising children in our faith, for support in face of challenges, and for new insights regarding the basic teachings of the Church.

He continued, explaining that thirty percent of parishioners appear to be 'Sunday Catholics' who look to the parish only for Sunday liturgy. Ten percent of parishioners participate in Sunday liturgy out of a spirit of obligation, "but the parish and Church today seem to be a source of frustration and discontent. Thirty percent of parishioners are parishioners in name only. These are the one or two times a year Catholics. This segment of the parish just doesn't seem to care one way or the other."

Catechetical ministry depends to a great extent on how the worshiping community views itself. Without the proper perspective, catechesis begins to suffer. "The parish is the people," and catechesis is part of the fabric of parish life. However, is it a small piece, a large swatch, or is it woven throughout in vibrant colors? How many members of the community does it touch? In this segment of the symposium process, the participants examined the life and activities of their parishes as part of this evaluation.

Synopsis

After the welcome and introductions on the morning of the first day, the participants were asked to review their responses for the first set of reflection questions. In order to facilitate discussion, the participants were seated at round tables, with five or six people per table. After a few minutes of reflection, the table groups reviewed the questions and spoke about their responses. Next, each group developed summary points and appointed a representative to a panel which, in turn, communicated these points to everyone in the room. At the completion of the panel presentations, the floor was open to discussion.

Reflection Questions

The reflection questions found at the beginning of the chapters are the ones the participants answered in preparation for the symposium. As you enter into this process, please take time for reflection and then answer the questions yourself.

What are your reflections about your parish? Take some time, gather your thoughts, and answer the questions on the next two pages.

☐☐ Reflection Questions
☐■ **The Parish**

What impact does your parish have:

- On the lives of parishioners?

- On the surrounding community?

- On the national or global community?

The Parish

☐☐ Reflection Questions
☐■ **The Parish** (continued)

How does family participation in the parish affect parish life?

Describe the mission of your parish. What are the three most important goals in the life and mission of the parish?

Responses from the symposium participants

What impact does your parish have on the lives of parishioners?

- The parish nurtures the faith of parishioners in terms of education and formation, worship, and prophetic challenge to live the Gospel message. We encourage them to support each other in finding God in their own struggles and busyness of family life as they are challenged with issues of justice and social responsibility.

- The parish is where people serve one another and bear the afflictions of one another. It is where one rediscovers the art of learning—adult literacy programs, basic ministry training, scripture groups, Christian formation, youth ministry. It is where one rediscovers God in the lives and prayers of the marginalized: drug users, prostitutes, gang members, the hungry and homeless, the sick, and the abused. Finally, our parish community is a people gathered to bring about change.

- The parish gives people a sense of belonging and participation. It draws the parishioners into learning more about their faith. It provides the education of the children, both religious education and academic education. It provides alternatives to gang activities. It gives them more awareness of their identity of life. It provides a forum for service to others. It helps them take ownership of their parish.

- The parish nourishes the faith of the parishioners in Christ Jesus. It has an extensive role in the formation of the faith—from the Catholic school program to the religious education program that together educate about 1400 students a year.

- Depending upon the degree of involvement of the parishioner, it is the religious center for all family members as well as the community and social center for extending relationships. For many, apart from work and the immediate family, it is the center of their lives. For those who are less involved, it is a center for immediate social service as well as a place of celebration for important events. These events bring in other family members and friends in time of crises, loss, and tragedy.

- The parish is the center of the community's life. In a small community, people look to the church for social as well as spiritual support.

- The parish is home to many recent immigrants who feel disconnected from their family and culture. In the parish they can speak their language and be understood. They can meet new friends who graciously welcome them to the neighborhood and assist them through the difficult process of adjustment to a new culture. More importantly, the parishioners celebrate their unique faith expression in a multicultural ambiance that respects and nurtures the Hispanic, Asian, African-American, and Anglo cultures.

- For many people the parish is the only visible link to God that they have in a very secular society. The parish offers people a place to come where they are unconditionally accepted.

NOTES

Impact of Parish

The participants spoke about ways their parishes are making an impact on parishioners, the surrounding community, and the national and global community. Communicating the insights of each table group by means of a panel discussion, the floor was opened to questions, comments, and additional observations once each member of the panel reported to the group. The result was a frank exchange of opinions and information. In order to provide organization for both the panel presentations and the observations that followed, and not to imply priority or importance, the ideas have been grouped according to the following categories:

- Pastors and Evolving Models of Parish
- Service to Parish and Community
- Service to Global Community
- Recognition of Limitations
- Empowerment of Lay Leadership

Pastors and Evolving Models of Parish

This community is based not on force or accident of geographic location or even on deeper ties of ethnic origin, but on the life of the Spirit which unites its members in a unique fellowship so intimate that Paul likens it to a body of which each individual is a part and Jesus Himself is the Head.
To Teach As Jesus Did, 22

During the symposium, the participants frequently referred to the Second Vatican Council and to the changes resulting from it. Many spoke of the excitement and energy with which they greeted the Council documents and the challenge of renewal. The approach of their ministry continues to reflect the spirit of this renewal. One priest spoke about the "tremendous theological change in my lifetime." He continued to say that Vatican II called people to take seriously the words of Jesus, 'Where two or three are gathered together in my name, there I am in their midst.' "And so if we want to find God it's no longer in the heavens, but it's within ourselves and within one another. And that's a drastic change." However, he believes it will be a long time before the majority of people make that change and see the presence of God in one another.

As the session and the discussions progressed, it became evident that the changes initiated by Vatican II were expanding the boundaries of what might be considered the usual parish organizational structure. Leadership, specifically the expectations of the people of the parish and the actual leadership style of the pastor, comprises one component of the changing dynamic. As an example, a participant offered two scenarios that might occur when a new priest comes into a parish. In the first, the people say: "It's your show, Father. What do you want us to do?" Whereas in the second, the people tell the new pastor: "This is who we are. This is our soul. Our past leadership has given us ownership of ministry, and this is what we want of you as our pastor to help continue to promote and enable us to be this." The discussions throughout the symposium illustrate a leadership style that reflects the second scenario.

One pastor believed the morning's discussions revealed that successful parishes tend toward a model which is not only organizational but clearly relational, and the success of this model may require a reexamination of some of the ways in which parishes operate. As a point of reference, he spoke of interfaith organizations that channel the energies of their member churches into community efforts. These groups do not begin their efforts attempting to organize people. They begin by getting people to talk with each other in a relational way, so people get to know each other and their common concerns.

Speaking of his experience with similar organizations, another pastor explained how small groups in his county worked together to alleviate a serious problem in the community and to secure the funding needed to carry out their program. A substantial effort began on a grass roots level. These examples reflect the synergy that is happening within the parishes. Applying this type of relational organization to small Christian communities, one priest spoke of developing a program for lay people that will be a system for organizing, sustaining, and training small group leaders and small group ministries.

Later, a priest remarked how in the past people joined their neighborhood parish. Today, with increasing frequency, when people do not feel comfortable with their neighborhood parish they travel to a parish which nurtures their faith and gives them a sense of belonging. He reflected that "we're still holding on to old models, whereas the people are saying well maybe the parish has to be rethought somewhat." A similar issue was addressed by another participant. "There's a tension between a model of church that focuses a lot on control and a model of church that says we have to empower and demands we give ownership. That is a tension. As to where it's going, I don't know. I can't do anything about it except empower as best as I can, both models."

The topic of success, its perception and measure, was also addressed by the group. One priest shared the observation that the Church may still operate out of a model that evaluates the success of a parish based on the percentage of people in church on a Sunday. He questioned the reliability of this as a sound measure of the impact of a parish. Instead, he believes it may be more important to look at the people who do come and participate in liturgy and feel that they are being affected greatly and that they in turn are affecting others.

For the symposium participants, it appears that models of parish are evolving as the pastors work to proclaim and live the mission of church as they envision it. Two pastors offered observations that spoke of this evolving model. One commented that the parishes that have life and are vibrant are the ones that have complemented a saving model with a serving model. These communities have a great sense of discipleship and stewardship, so they position their energies and abilities in the service of others. He continued to say that when parishioners become good stewards and effective disciples, a parish is filled with life.

The power of witness in these parishes was recognized by another pastor. "I think that I am hearing that the focus in the parish is not one of indoctrination, but rather one of demonstration. Christianity is being demonstrated. No one is

NOTES

trying to convince anybody of Christianity, but rather they're about the business of witnessing Christianity by their actions." This reflects a statement made by Pope Paul VI in *Evangelii Nuntiandi*: "As we said recently to a group of lay people, 'Modern man listens more willingly to witnesses than to teachers, and if he does listen to teachers, it is because they are witnesses.'" (*Evangelii Nuntiandi*, 41)

Another priest reported that the participants at his table also found that parishes that are alive are the ones that have a strong sense of discipleship and stewardship. "I think we found that same thing, we found different levels of that." He continued to say that in all the parish communities examined in the group's discussion, people are identifying the Church with service. The examples and responses offered throughout the symposium point to parishes that strongly emphasize parishioner service, responsibility, and formation.

Reflection

How strong is the sense of discipleship in your parish? What are some ways you could help this develop?

Service to Parish and Community

As early as the patristic age, Saint Ambrose and Saint John Chrysostom—to quote only them—gave prominence to the social consequences of the demands made by the Gospel.
Catechesi Tradendae, 29

The importance of stewardship and discipleship in the life of the parish was evident throughout the discussions. Also evident was the commitment to develop and empower lay leadership to be disciples who serve with conviction.

Services offered by the parishes represented at the symposium go beyond traditional catechetical and sacramental programs. These parishes reach out to people in the spirit of the gospel message of justice and peace. The diverse types of experience varied from food pantries and soup kitchens to helping undocumented farm workers and gang counseling. As stated by the *National Catechetical Directory*, "to be a sign of God's kingdom already here, the Church on every level—most immediately on the parish level—must be committed to justice, love, and peace, to grace and holiness, truth and life, for these are the hallmarks of the kingdom of God." (*NCD*, 67)

The *National Catechetical Directory* also gives a name to this type of work: stewardship. "Adults need to learn and practice the gospel demands of stewardship: God gives everyone a measure of personal time, talent, and treasure to use for His glory and the service of neighbor." (*NCD*, 188) Evangelization provides the underlying factor for this approach to stewardship and discipleship. Adopting a familiar saying, one pastor said: "It is easier for people to act their way into a new manner of thinking than think their way into a new manner of acting. So in terms of converting people, actual contact and involvement is much more powerful than preaching at them."

The discussion can be categorized according to the groups being served:

- Parishioners
- Families
- Newcomers
- Community

Parishioners

One table group described the parish as being a very welcoming place. The people's presence on Sunday was often the only chance to touch their lives, and so this effort would begin with welcoming them at the door and would continue welcoming in the liturgy, as well as in the ministry of the entire parish life. The individuals in this group saw great effort being put into their parishes to energize them so they would be welcoming and supportive.

The parishes represented at another table were primarily small and rural. For them, the parish represents more than just the spiritual center of their lives. It also provides a social setting for people to get to know one another, and it is the location for many community activities. "My parish is 80% undocumented farm workers. If the Catholic church were not present there, there would be no place where Anglo ranchers and their farm workers can get together in a mutual setting of support. The faith is the only thing they have in common."

NOTES

Another speaker referred to organizations, mentioned earlier, that effectively link parishes in practical ways to achieve certain goals. He explained that normally his parishioners only think about their own parish. Once they become involved with a broader organization, they begin to meet people from other parishes in order to work on larger issues. At the same time he recognizes a need to continue to develop the smaller communities "where people can know each other by name, where they find support, where they find healing."

Families

The importance of the family in parish life resounded clearly through all the responses. Families constitute a focal point, both as providers and beneficiaries. Three excerpts from the participants' reflection question responses express this importance from slightly different perspectives. The first offers creative ways to involve the entire family in the liturgical celebration, the second raises a potential challenge, and the third embraces an expanded definition of family.

- "Family involvement has great importance in this parish. We have a Family Choir—consisting of moms, dads, and kids of all ages. Our Ministers of Hospitality at Sunday liturgies include whole families doing the greeting, welcoming, collection, and good-byes at the door."

- "Although the parish has a nice range of age groups, the majority of those who are active and involved in various activities, etc., are families. It seems that families bring energy, life, enthusiasm to the parish. It is also apparent that much of our programming for religious education and social activities is directed to families. Much of our parish resources and personnel goes to meet the spiritual and educational needs of families. It is a plus to have vibrant, energized and committed families. It is also a curse in that other age groups and needs may be overlooked or relegated to a lower level of concern."

- "Much of our parish life is oriented towards serving families. However, we are increasingly aware of the need to minister to extended families, to single parent families, to broken or hurting homes, and to young adults. Our parish is growing older so we are devoting increasing attention to the elderly, especially those who are alone or shut-in."

Newcomers

The parishes provide a warm Christian welcome to the people or communities who are looking for help. In the case of people coming into the country, it is essential that the parish be "a welcoming community and provide those people with a hope of new beginnings."

One group reported that each person at the table came from a parish with distinctly different congregations that had differing sets of needs. One had a large immigrant community to whom the parish represented safety. One had a Cajun community, for whom the parish offered comfort and welcome for all. Another came from a suburban parish. Then there was a parish comprised predominantly of the upper middle class, for whom the parish was the center of life. Finally, a cathedral community was represented.

In reviewing these diverse situations, the group saw a response to need, whether that need be literacy, a sense of place for things to happen, or a place to address some of the community concerns. This response to need gives people a sense of belonging, and hence a bond with the parish. Therefore pastors have to identify the concerns of their parishioners "and give some space and room for people to develop. In the process of that, we see people growing in confidence."

In the midst of this, methods of service are evolving. For example, a pastor explained how parishioners from wealthy communities are beginning to be challenged to have truly hands-on experience. "Like at Christmas time, not just to send money to people who don't have enough, but to celebrate Christmas with them. Having a meal with them and realizing what they really ought to offer is not so much what they have in excess materially, but what they have in abundance spiritually."

Not only can parishioners offer from their spiritual abundance, they are also touched by the wealth of spirituality of the people they serve. Though the following citation from *Gaudium et Spes* refers to nations, the truth applies for a family or an individual. "Filled with wisdom man is led through visible realities to those which cannot be seen. . . . It should also be pointed out that many nations, poorer as far as material goods are concerned yet richer as regards wisdom, can be of the greatest advantage to others." (*Gaudium et Spes*, 15)

Community

The parishes of the participants frequently supplement services offered by the local community or provide services not available in the community, reaching out to both parishioners and non-parishioners. Referring to the parish, one participant said: "It doesn't serve only the registered parishioners. It's a community building experience in a place where people are arriving from all kinds of places." One of the objectives set by *Go and Make Disciples* is "To involve parishes and local service groups in the needs of their neighborhood." (*Go and Make Disciples*, page 19)

Responses to the reflection questions detailed various ways in which the parishes serve the community. Many participants referred to food pantries, clothing store-rooms, and services for support groups. The following responses list additional examples of community involvement.

- Two staff members are members of the school district's student Academic Review Board.

- The parish is involved in the "Hope in Youth" Campaign to combat the gang problem in the community, and is a vehicle for other community service programs.

- The parish is an active member of a private non-profit organization composed of parishes, congregations, synagogues, unions, employee groups, and community groups. Working at the grass roots level, it develops local leaders and empowers citizens to build basic civic and family life consistent with Judeo-Christian and democratic values.

The Parish

NOTES

- The parish organizes youth activities for youth of all religious affiliations. Surrounding communities check with the parish before scheduling youth activities.
- The parish provides a focal point for Catholics as well as non-Catholics through:
    - various workshops (finding employment, writing résumés, etc.)
    - a special collection each Sunday to assist the ministry of local agencies working to curb homelessness, hunger, illiteracy, etc.
    - an ongoing relationship with Habitat for Humanity.
- The parish worked with several churches and the United Way to open a shelter for battered families.
- The parochial school provides a good education in a city with a poor and unsafe educational setting.
- The parish provides open gymnasium hours for the community, resources and meeting space for Al-Anon, Girl Scouts, Boy Scouts, Red Cross and other community organizations. In time of civil emergency the parish serves as a shelter for the community.
- The parish and a number of Protestant Churches provide food once a month for 500 families. The parish has a Community Store that provides clothing for low income families.

Reflection

How does your parish respond to meet social justice needs?

Impact If Closed

During this discussion the following question was raised: "If your parish were closed tomorrow by the bishop for whatever reason, who besides the registered Catholics would miss it?" The responses fell into two areas: moral leadership and social services provided.

Moral Leadership

Many participants pointed to the impact that their parishes have on the people of the local communities. As one pastor explained: "We are living in a society with certain values which are very consumer oriented." He said parishes are ecologically minded, are pro-life, have integrated schools, show the enrichment of different national groups, respect national cultures, and bring diverse groups together, such as ranchers and workers. "All of that is creating a kind of a Christian counter-cultural approach to life in this society."

Offering another example, one pastor referred to the emphasis that the Catholic Church places on the sacrament of marriage. He said the Church offers pre-Cana, Engaged Encounter, Marriage Encounter, and ministries to divorced and separated. For the most part, these are conducted by lay people. Another said the Catholic Church is a force for social change. He pointed to the leadership of the Church in the 60's and 70's that helped to bring about confrontation with racial prejudice. Others spoke of the impact the parishes have on people who can influence the environments of business, education, and civic government.

Finally, a priest whose parish includes a large immigrant population explained that a bilingual parish gives a witness to the community, "a witness to the local government that the Spanish speaking people [or other non-English speaking people] are a large and needful group." Worshiping together gives the people a heightened visible presence and identity.

Social Services

Several priests also identified services that would be curtailed if their parishes no longer existed. With the emphasis on stewardship in many parishes, their closing would have a negative impact on the food and clothing given to the poor. Service provided to pregnant young women through the work in Birthright would be disrupted. Parents who have children in daycare would have to find other help for their children. One pastor explained that in an effort to be good stewards, the parish gives away 30% of its budget annually, so there would be an ensuing ripple effect. Another pointed to the outreach and care given to people with AIDS. The parish school, as an alternative to public education, would also be missed.

In addition to the specific services provided by the parishes, a pastor said an important outlet for civic services would also be removed. "Everyone in our group provided some kind of social outreach to the community. For those of us who network with civic or secular organizations to distribute or to provide services, the impact would be great because we can provide those services in a family setting, in a place where people feel comfortable to receive the

The Parish

NOTES

services of the state. They don't feel that [comfort] if they were to go to another agency. It would be a big impact on pride and dignity and all the things we are able to offer that others can't."

Another person added that his parish is a refuge for the homeless, the hungry, prostitutes, and drug users, where they know they can be who they are without being branded. As Jesus reached out to the lepers, prostitutes, and tax collectors, the parish can reach out and minister to groups that others may shun.

Reflection

If your parish were to close, who besides the registered Catholics would miss it?

Service to National and Global Communities

"Any other commandment [is] summed up in this sentence: 'You shall love your neighbor as yourself...' therefore love is the fulfilling of the law." (Rom. 13:9–10) It goes without saying that this is a matter of the utmost importance to men who are coming to rely more and more on each other and to a world which is becoming more unified every day.
Gaudium et Spes, 24

The relation between some parishes and the national and global communities can be seen from a few responses to the reflection questions.

- A social justice group raises awareness and serves the poor and supports those who do, i.e., Campaign for Human Development, and all other diocesan missionary and relief efforts.

- A parish helped relief efforts for the flood victims in Tijuana by monetary donations and by transporting food, medicine, blankets, and clothing.

- The parish is part of greater efforts, such as national pro-life marches.

- The Social Action for Peace and Justice Committee brings issues of concern to the attention of the parish and provides ways of enlightening elected representatives as to its position.

The participants offered additional ways in which their parishes reach out to the global community. One pastor takes groups to Haiti to help them gain a first hand understanding of the problems there. A parish bought a tractor for people in Nigeria, while another raised money to build housing for teachers in Kenya. Many referred to their support of missions. And as one participant explained, parishes with any immigrant community can in some way affect the country of origin of the people in that community.

When asked what they did to help people in their parishes see that they are part of a global community, participants responded that two important methods are the homily and adult formation.

A participant explained that the priests seated at his table represented parishes that have military bases and state colleges within their boundaries. Their parishioners also include CEO's who are in charge of international companies. Therefore, they use the homily to convey ideas that will have an impact on the people present—people who eventually go to the Pentagon, CEO's who eventually work with executives from other countries, and college professors who teach students. These parishioners can influence the people they meet. As expressed by the pastor: "I guess what it says is don't slop your Sunday sermon away. Make sure it is a value for people to hear."

Another pastor said his parish sponsors a program for high school students to help them understand the differences in cultures and the experiences of living in another culture. Another parish, with two large immigrant populations, organizes events involving the two groups so they can work together and get to know each other. According to one priest, a real impact will not happen until attitudes and lifestyles change so that no longer will 20% of the world's people use 80% of its resources. His parish works to conserve resources.

NOTES

The participants were asked whether they have been or are pastors of a parish that has a twinning relationship with another parish outside the United States. More than half the priests responded affirmatively.

An example of service to the global community was offered by one of the priests. "I spent a sabbatical in Tanzania with the Maryknollers and in Ethiopia with CRS. Before I left on sabbatical the parishioners gave me $16,000 to take with me to Africa, because they knew that I would be on the scene and they knew the money would get to people who needed it. Likewise the parish I'm in now, we have a sister parish in Guatemala and a sister parish in our own inner city." He further explained that parish groups have visited Guatemala, and groups from the Guatemalan parish have visited them.

However, participants also recognized obstacles to nurturing a global view on the part of the parish. As one person wrote in a reflection question response: "[My parishioners] see little relationship between faith and citizenship, national or world. My members do not see church beyond the walls of the structure. Younger members are so focused on family that little time or resource is left for such a larger focus. Service to environment and poor is left to a very small 'aware' group of parishioners. However, ministry and holiday service projects always secure a very positive response. I sense we are a community that could, in time, truly respond to the call to service of nation and world."

Reflection

In what ways does your parish address national and global issues? What are some obstacles to your parish's recognition of its part in the national and global communities?

Recognition of Limitations

During the morning's discussions, one pastor voiced a concern. "Everything seems so perfect. My experience is that it isn't." As an example, he said in his parish there is a little bit of concern for global world vision, but a limited group of people sustain that interest. The consciousness of the average parishioner still has to be touched by something that affects them much more directly. Though many good things were being said at the symposium, he saw them as little lights. For him, parish life can be very demanding and tiring at the same time. Usually there is success some areas, but not in all areas.

Another pastor responded: "The question before us today is: 'What impact are we having?' If you had asked me where are we failing I'd give you a longer list. I really believe this very sincerely. I think we spend too much time bemoaning what we are not doing and not recognizing the good the Lord permits us to do. That was the question today: What are we doing?"

In many cases the pastors provide the vision and leadership, at least initially. However, someone stated that pastors may also need guidance in this area. He explained that although there are a tremendous number of talented pastors across the country, they sometimes need a source of vision in order to organize and give focus to their ministries and what they are trying to accomplish in this environment. "Some people can generate that for themselves, but most people really need help to do that."

Reflection

Who are the people and what are the materials that you can look to as resources?

NOTES

Empowerment of Lay Leadership

The degree of empowerment by these pastors is striking. Although the topic of the symposium sought to examine ways in which pastors empower catechists, these pastors actively seek to empower lay leadership at all levels of parish ministry.

One participant reported that he and some others were puzzled that the focus of this symposium was the priest as an empowerer. However, from listening to one another's experience, it became very clear to them just how critical pastors are to the parish. "From the examples that were shared around the table, ministry happened or didn't happen because of the pastor." He referred to a sentiment expressed by a college rector who explained that how a group feels about itself comes from the top down and how much a group gets done comes from the bottom up.

Another pastor spoke about the development of lay leadership and how he then allows "the people to have ownership of the parish. To realize that the parish was theirs as much as it was his." He explained that to accomplish this, a priest must have good listening skills. He must not only listen to what the people say, but must move the people to take action themselves.

After hearing this, one participant wondered what would happen if that parish were to close tomorrow? The response was: "I suspect they would go on. . . . None of the programs depend upon me except to give them money. But otherwise the administration of them depends upon others, and I suspect they would even be able to get the money if they really had to." Another pastor added that a few years ago his current parish had to face the possibility of closing. The parishioners decided they would do all that was necessary to continue being a parish, and sound lay participation in the conduct of the parish's affairs has kept them together. Another group spoke about people in parish ministry who had been formed as leaders and who in turn formed others.

However, positive results do not need to be measured in large numbers. One priest said there are many levels of commitment, even on the parish's staff. He is very happy if he impacts twelve people and really helps them to grow and they help him to grow. In his mind, that is a major success. Another pastor said: "I know my limitations, and I discover people who are much better at handling situations and people than I can. And on the parish level that's a kind of ministry."

One participant said his parish has a vibrant liturgical and sacramental life, which is a key element of formation for the people. To ensure that all liturgical ministries are well-organized and have full participation, the parish helps parishioners develop ministerial leadership—as ministers in catechetics, in liturgy, and in service programs. The parish also has an extensive youth program, beyond that of catechetics, which tries to tie in the life of the younger parishioners to the parish and to the values of the Church.

Reflection

To what extent do the lay people in your parish assume leadership roles in parish ministry? How do you promote this leadership?

NOTES

NOTES

Summary

One of the facilitators observed that the morning session was a compelling affirmation that catechetical ministry depends to a great extent on how the worshiping community views itself. "Clearly, without having asked you what you do as catechists, you began by telling us what you do as priests in empowering the community." A description of the parishes of the participants and their approach to people and ministry includes the following points:

- The parishes provide the environment in which the people of God can come together as a community of faith.

- The vigor and vision of the parish depend on several factors, but should always be focused on the Church's mission of catechesis and evangelization.

- The parishes demonstrate a strong discipleship model. Pastors develop lay leaders and empower them to make parish ministries their own.

- The parishes display a strong sense of stewardship. Parishioners apply their time, skills, and money to serve God and neighbor, providing witness to the tenets of Christianity. These works embrace parishioners and non-parishioners, at times supplementing services provided by government. Absence of the parish would deprive the neighboring community not only of service, but of significant moral leadership.

- The parishes seek to increase awareness and involvement in national issues.

- Many parishes actively participate in service to the global community. More than half have a twinning relationship with a parish in another country.

- The pastors work with and help the laity to grow in faith. A critical avenue for this is the Sunday liturgy which includes a well-prepared homily.

The Next Step

The next segment examines Catechesis in the Parish. Before you continue, review your notes, reflections, and responses to questions in the segment on the Parish.

Take some time to answer the questions on the next two pages. The responses will help you complete the planning segment in Chapter 6.

☐☐ Planning Notes
☐■ **The Parish**

Identify the positive things you are doing in your parish. What are your strengths?

After reading the section on the parish, what may be areas of potential change or addition?

What are some thoughts about strengthening existing programs?

What are some resources for change—people, material, programs?

What are some obstacles to change? How can you overcome them?

Chapter 2
Catechesis in the Parish

NOTES

Introduction

As the twentieth century draws to a close, the Church is bidden by God and by events—each of them a call from him—to renew her trust in catechetical activity as a prime aspect of her mission. She is bidden to offer catechesis her best resources in people and energy, without sparing effort, toil or material means, in order to organize it better and to train qualified personnel.
Catechesi Tradendae, 15

What emphasis should a parish place on catechesis? What emphasis *does* a parish place on catechesis? What are some of the ways a parish shows this emphasis? The preceding quotation from the apostolic exhortation of Pope John Paul II provides a beginning focus.

Sharing the Light of Faith: National Catechetical Directory for Catholics of the United States (*NCD*) offers other elements when it explains that "catechesis is a lifelong process for the individual and a constant and concerted pastoral activity of the Christian community" (*NCD*, 32) and that becoming more Christlike "involves establishing and nurturing a real relationship to Jesus and the Father in the Holy Spirit, through a vigorous sacramental life, prayer, study, and serving others." (*NCD*, 173) All members of the Church are called to develop and strengthen their loving relationship with God throughout their lifetime, and they are called to help others do the same.

One of the most visible components of catechesis often is organized parish programs, "an education of children, young people and adults in the faith, which includes especially the teaching of Christian doctrine imparted, generally speaking, in an organic and systematic way, with a view to initiating the hearers into the fullness of Christian life." (*Catechesi Tradendae*, 18) Many people think of catechesis primarily in terms of catechetical and sacramental preparation programs for children. However, the early Christians saw catechesis as "the whole of the efforts within the Church to make disciples" (*Catechesi Tradendae*, 1), and this same vision remains valid today.

Though some people may see such programs as the most visible manifestation of catechesis, catechesis flows through all aspects of parish life. Of these, the liturgy is preeminent. As the *National Catechetical Directory* explains, "[catechesis] prepares people for full and active participation in liturgy (by helping them understand its nature, rituals, and symbols) and at the same time flows from liturgy, inasmuch as, reflecting upon the community's experiences of worship, it seeks to relate them to daily life and to growth in faith." (*NCD*, 113)

Catechesis goes beyond programs, beyond the liturgy. Catechesis is an essential source of life and energy for the other major ministries of the parish. The *National Catechetical Directory* states that catechesis has four interrelated purposes: "to proclaim the mysteries of the faith; to foster community; to encourage worship and prayer; and to motivate service to others." (*NCD*, 227)

NOTES

Every activity of the parish should have as its ultimate goal the message of bringing people closer to Jesus, strengthening their love of God so they willingly and enthusiastically share their love and their faith with others. This may be within a family, within a peer group, or at a community meeting.

The responsibility for parish catechesis is not limited to priests, DRE's, and designated volunteers. Each member of the parish community has a catechetical responsibility. And as part of this responsibility, each member must in turn be catechized continually. As one participant reflected, the connection and synergy of evangelization and catechesis comprise the dynamic that drives a parish. Both catechesis and evangelization are the task of the whole parish.

Synopsis

After having examined the overall life of the parish, the participants reviewed the role that catechesis plays in parish life. The session began with an exercise in which the participants defined their understanding of catechesis. Next, using this as a foundation, the participants reexamined their parish goals and mission statements in light of catechesis. This was first done individually and then the table groups reviewed how these goals affect the impact and implementation of catechesis in the parish. The groups recorded the key points of their discussion on flip charts, and later shared these points with the entire assembly. This chapter will take you through the same process.

Following the initial discussion of catechesis, one of the priests noted that in their brief definitions of catechesis the participants uniformly used "catechesis" rather than "religious education." These two terms are frequently used interchangeably. In fact, in the original symposium agenda, this section was titled "Catechesis/Religious Education in the Parish." Several reflection questions were similarly phrased. This was done because of the usage overlap as well as to be sure to draw upon experiences the participants may have had with varieties of parish programs, such as catechetical programs, schools, and others.

Although the terms "catechesis" and "religious education" are connected, they are different. There are important meanings attributed to each. For ease of reading, the headings and the text will primarily use the term "catechesis." The term "religious education" will be used when it reflects the language of the participants.

Reflection Questions

To prepare for this chapter, please take some time to respond to the questions on the next two pages. Some of the participants' responses to the reflection questions follow the questions and appear throughout the text. As you read the chapter, continue to consider the symposium discussions a benchmark for comparison with your responses. Engage in a dialogue with your catechetical associates. You can also engage in a mental dialogue with the symposium participants, framing your own responses in reaction to those of the participants.

☐☐ Reflection Questions
■■ **Catechesis in the Parish**

Reflect on your understanding of catechesis.

How does catechesis influence the life and mission of the parish? What priority does it have in relation to other parish ministries? What role does it play within other parish ministries?

☐☐ Reflection Questions
■■ **Catechesis in the Parish** (Continued)

What specific actions are taken to inform the parish community at large about its catechetical role and responsibilities?

What specific actions are taken to identify and/or enhance the catechetical role and responsibilities of families?

Responses from the symposium participants

How does catechesis affect the life and mission of the parish?

- Life is the constant journey towards God. Catechesis and religious education are the supplies for the journey. Without good supplies, you won't have a good journey.

- Catechesis is one of the fundamental priorities in the life of the parish.

- Catechesis calls the parish to awareness of identity as members of a parish. The parish seeks to have a life as community of worship and service. Formation offers light on that experience. It prepares people for the sacramental life and involves them in the celebration of liturgy. Catechesis offers people an experience of community and invites people into the service of the parish community and the larger community.

- Since catechesis is viewed as a formation process, it plays a key role in the life and mission of our parish. Leadership in all other ministries comes from an effective catechetical ministry and lay formation. It is through parish leadership that the parish's mission is more clearly articulated and carried out.

- If catechesis doesn't affect family life—whatever fundamental relationships that circle of intimacy may entail—it is not really successful.

- The task of religious education today is to present the basic truths of faith in such a way that people apply them to their lives. Catechesis needs to be an invitation from committed and faith filled individuals to others, inviting them into the sacred, gracious mystery of God's love.

    Catechesis influences the life and mission of the parish to the degree that parishioners accept the truth that all of us are teachers, all of us are bearers of the Good News. What we are trying to do in the parish is to emphasize the commitment made at baptism to be proclaimers and livers of the truth about Jesus and God.

- The pastoral ministry and vision of a catechizing parish influences all of the parish activity.

- It is the heart and life blood of the parish and its mission.

NOTES

What is Catechesis?

"What language would you use to describe catechesis in your parish?" The responses of the participants, spontaneous and brief descriptions of catechesis, were recorded on flip charts and remained displayed throughout the symposium. These responses appear on the next page, and fuller references from recent documents of the Church are listed on page 36. Before you review them, take a few moments to reflect on *your* concept of catechesis, and then record the words or phrases that capture this concept. You may want to paper clip this page so as you work through the rest of this book, you can easily turn back to your definition of catechesis for reference or revision.

As I understand it, catechesis is:

Responses from the symposium participants

Catechesis is:

- Development of people's faith
- Formation
- Passing on a sacred story
- Reflection on our faith
- Empowering people
- Passing on the good news
- Helping people to surrender their hearts to the love of God
- Part of a total ministry of the word of God. You have to see it also together with evangelization and homiletics.
- One of our ministries of spirituality
- Demonstrating Christianity
- A rooting of people in their relationship with God
- Characterized by the interlocking dimensions of message, community, worship, and service
- Lifelong
- Rooting
- A process that gives form to the faith
- Pointing to the sacred in our midst and inviting people into that
- Central to the life of the parish community
- Discovering God
- The source of other ministries
- Passing on Catholic traditions
- Trying to put mystery into concrete terms
- Where faith and life meet
- Sharing faith experiences and developing Christian values
- A task with the ministry of the whole parish
- User friendly
- Introducing people to Jesus, then to Christianity, then to Catholicism, not the other way around
- Lifelong, on-going process
- Going into the origin of the word, drawing the best out of people
- Making them familiar with scripture and the tradition of the church
- Directed to adults in faith
- Relational to liturgy and service

NOTES

> *Selected references about catechesis from Church documents*
>
> - Catechesis refers to efforts which help individuals and communities acquire and deepen Christian faith and identity through initiation rites, instruction, and formation of conscience. It includes both the message presented and the way in which it is presented.
>   *National Catechetical Directory*, 5
>
> - The specific aim of catechesis is to develop, with God's help, an as yet initial faith, and to advance in fullness and to nourish day by day the Christian life of the faithful, young and old. . . . Catechesis aims therefore at developing understanding of the mystery of Christ in the light of God's word, so that the whole of a person's humanity is impregnated by that word.
>   *Catechesi Tradendae*, 20
>
> - Bishops should also endeavor to use the various methods available nowadays for proclaiming Christian doctrine. There are, first of all, preaching and catechetical instruction, which will always hold pride of place.
>   *Christus Dominus*, 13
>
> - Chief among these is catechetical instruction, which illumines and strengthens the faith, develops a life in harmony with the spirit of Christ, stimulates a conscious and fervent participation in the liturgical mystery and encourages men to take an active part in the apostolate.
>   *Declaration on Christian Education*, 4
>
> - While not being formally identified with them, catechesis is built on a certain number of elements of the Church's pastoral mission which have a catechetical aspect, that prepare for catechesis, or spring from it. They are: the initial proclamation of the Gospel or missionary preaching to arouse faith; examination of the reasons for belief; experience of Christian living; celebration of the sacraments; integration into the ecclesial community; and apostolic and missionary witness.
>   *Catechism of the Catholic Church*, 6
>
> - Catechesis seeks to move people to live justly, mercifully, and peacefully as individuals, to act as the leaven of the gospel in family, school, work, social, and civic life, and to work for appropriate social change.
>   *NCD*, 170.9
>
> - Family catechesis precedes, accompanies, and enriches other forms of instruction in the faith.
>   *Catechism of the Catholic Church*, 2226
>
> - Very soon the name of catechesis was given to the whole of the efforts within the Church to make disciples, to help people to believe that Jesus is the Son of God, so that believing they might have life in his name, and to educate and instruct them in this life and thus build up the Body of Christ.
>   (about the early Church) *Catechesi Tradendae*, 1
>
> - . . . postbaptismal catechesis . . . is a time for the community and the neophytes together to grow in deepening their grasp of the paschal mystery and in making it part of their lives through meditation on the Gospel, sharing the eucharist, and doing the works of charity.
>   *Rite of Christian Initiation of Adults*, 244

An understanding of how members of the parish perceive catechesis and the role that it plays in the parish is obviously pivotal to this process. Based on their responses, catechesis to the participants appears to be rooted in the total parish experience. It is a lifelong process, central to the life of the parish, that has the interlocking dimensions of message, worship, community, and service. The responses seemed to be rooted in the experience of catechesis in the parish. Later, one of the pastors commented that none of these spontaneous responses focused exclusively on children. The participants viewed catechesis as a lifelong development of faith. Catechesis may begin with children, but it continues through all ages of the person. Indeed, appropriate catechesis is the right of all believers and members of the parish.

Important Goals in the Life and Mission of the Parish

As the next step in examining the role of catechesis in their parishes, the participants returned to their reflection question booklets and reviewed the mission statement and major goals of the parish, which were qualified as "the stated goals publicized to the parishioners." After this individual review, the people compared, contrasted, and examined this information with the others at their tables.

Before continuing, review the parish goals that you recorded in the reflection questions for Chapter 1: The Parish. Next, compare your parish goals with those listed by the participants. Many of these appear on the following two pages. Though the priests represented communities of vastly differing complexions, their goals are similar.

If the goals of the participants had to be distilled into five main areas, they would probably be akin to the ones listed by this pastor:

- Well-planned and life-giving liturgies.
- A sense of community and family as part and parcel of the parish.
- Leadership and ministerial development for parishioners.
- A continuous desire to keep the parish aware of the needs of the poor and the issues of social concern.
- A sense of the importance of evangelization, especially through the rites of the RCIA and the awareness of that process.

NOTES

Responses from the symposium participants

Important goals in the life and mission of the parish:

- Full, active, and conscious participation in worship

    Christian formation: catechetical ministry for children, youth, young adults; adult formation, initiation, leadership development

    Community growth and involvement

- Evangelization through RCIA, and Catholic movements, and organizations

    Religious education for all ages

    Worship and liturgy that brings the parish community together. Liturgies that deepen faith, strengthen our unity in Christ, and empower our parishioners to Christian witness in society and to serve those in need

- The spiritual development of parishioners

    A way to meet and support parishioners in sharing and promoting their Christian values to each other and our society

    To educate our parishioners at all ages in the tradition of the Church and ways in which the gospel can be applied to their present circumstances

- Faith

    Celebration

    Community

    Service

- To increase our efforts to evangelize and increase the number of those attending Sunday Mass

    To promote unity between the Spanish speaking and English speaking communities

    To be the Catholic presence in the area. To make ourselves and our faith visible in the community

- To increase involvement in quality liturgical celebrations of the sacraments

    To reach out with hospitality and love to our parishioners and beyond in service to the needy

    To improve our understanding of the gospel and Jesus' message (from womb to tomb) and apply it to the complexities of modern life

- Building unity within our diversity

    Being challenged by the word and nourished by the eucharist

    Educating ourselves and others in the ways of the Gospel

Catechesis in the Parish

NOTES

Responses from the symposium participants

Important goals in the life and mission of the parish:

- Individual growth, maturity and holiness

  Community growth, acceptance and development

  To be of service to others in the community

- To celebrate liturgies that "connect" with the lives of the people

  To provide a quality program that imparts a vision of the Kingdom of God to the participants so that the values of the Kingdom can be seen more clearly

  To call people to ministry and to equip them for ministry

- Liturgy—without good liturgy people won't come back for anything else.

  Youth—without good education and youth ministry the church of tomorrow will be crippled by the mistakes of today.

- Worship: As we develop, the worship life of the parish seems to be the area of greatest intensity.

  Education: A goal for the future would be the faith formation of all ages—too long neglected in the church of our area.

  Community: In some ways, the basis of the first two! Since the parish population is so large, new approaches must be developed to create some sense of belonging and ownership.

- To work toward a greater understanding and appreciation for the personal and communal experience of God in the sacraments and other liturgical prayer

  To promote a deeper appreciation for the importance of family where we are known, loved, and accepted; to provide ministry within all phases of the family life cycles

  To develop a sense of leadership, responsibility, and identity within our faith community by a process of education and formation for all parishioners at every age and stage of development

  To form a cohesive and caring parish community which shares Christ's presence with others, both within the Church and in the larger society

  To develop a well defined plan to maintain and improve the physical plant and grounds of our parish

  To create a greater understanding of stewardship and the responsibilities it implies in time, talent and treasure

- Our goal is to make everyone aware of what it means to be the Church and then challenge all to live that truth. In our mission statement we call ourselves "A people with the mission of Christ."

NOTES

Reflection

Once the participants reviewed their goals and mission statements, they were asked to examine two sets of questions which covered the impact and implementation of catechesis. The first set included:

- How does catechesis impact the parish mission or goals?
- How does catechesis impact the other ministries in the parish?
- How does catechesis impact parishioners?

Then, the second question was:

- How do the community and families carry out their catechetical role?

Consider these questions in light of your parish's mission and experience.

Categories

After sharing responses to the questions listed on the previous page, a representative from each group reported the key points from the table discussions. As with any discussion, some points were repeated, while others were made by only one person or group. However, there were distinct trends. To report these clearly and with structure, the information has been organized into four categories:

- Ministry of the Word
- The Woven Fabric of Catechesis
- Adult Directed Catechesis
- Family as Primary Catechist

Ministry of the Word

The ministry of the Word, too—pastoral preaching, catechetics and all forms of Christian instruction, among which the liturgical homily should hold pride of place—is healthily nourished and thrives in holiness through the Word of Scripture.

Dei Verbum, 24

The participants continually emphasized the role of the word. One pastor wrote that the ministry of the word—evangelization, catechesis, and preaching —is basic and essential to fostering a living and active faith. Another explained that, in his parish, catechesis "is a continuation of the Sunday scriptures, the homily, etc., and a concrete application to the events of the parishioners' daily lives."

Throughout the symposium, participants repeatedly referred to the role of the homily in catechesis and the impact that it has. One priest spoke particularly eloquently about its importance. "My experience is that the homily has potential to awaken in people, tap into people, that hunger that can lead them to further catechesis. . . . I can't think of liturgy without the word, . . . the few moments that we have with the people have the potential to awaken in them a thirst for the word and for growth and for life which is Jesus."

He also wrote about this in response to a reflection question. "Being in the heart of the Bible Belt you learn very quickly how significant the Sunday worship service is to people. As many as 70% of our couples are interfaith. These people come with real expectations of the worship experience. Preaching has for many become as important as the Eucharist. Because of the large number of Protestants, occasions such as weddings and funerals become opportunities for evangelization when the liturgies are done well."

This concern reflects the statement Pope John Paul II makes about the homily in *Catechesi Tradendae*. "Much attention must be given to the homily: it should be neither too long nor too short; it should always be carefully prepared, rich in substance and adapted to the hearers, and reserved to ordained ministers. The homily should have its place not only in every Sunday and feast-day Eucharist, but also in the celebration of baptisms, penitential liturgies, marriages and funerals." (*Catechesi Tradendae*, 48)

NOTES

Another pastor expressed belief that the community is formed by the word, and so the value of praying the word must become a priority. He explained that reflection before and during Mass opens up the value of formation at all levels. He also expressed a hope that small communities gather around the word as a focus of formation. He sees these as including parish committees, ministry groups, and social groups.

During the discussion, one pastor told the group that the priority of the word is foundational to everything else. He explained that the priests at his table shared examples that illustrated how other religious denominations devote considerable energy to the word and are very effective in their ministry. The participant believes that this importance must be emphasized "without taking anything away from liturgy, or the integration of the word into liturgy."

These observations about the power of the word reflect Canon 528 §1. "The pastor is obliged to see to it that the word of God in its entirety is announced to those living in the parish; for this reason he is to see to it that the lay Christian faithful are instructed in the truths of the faith, especially through the homily which is to be given on Sundays and holy days of obligation and through the catechetical formation which he is to give; he is to foster works by which the spirit of the gospel, including issues involving social justice, is promoted; he is to take special care for the Catholic education of children and of young adults; he is to make every effort with the aid of the Christian faithful to bring the gospel message also to those who have ceased practicing their religion or who do not profess the true faith." (*Code of Canon Law*, 528 §1)

Reflection

How do the homilies in your parish catechize? What impact do the homilies have? How are parishioners encouraged to provide input or evaluation?

The Woven Fabric of Catechesis

A weaving image conveys an approach to catechesis shared by the participants. They do not view catechesis as a distinct component of the church community. Rather, it is woven throughout all activities, strengthening and coloring the fabric of parish life. "Every aspect of parish life is seen to have a catechetical component, minimally as a way to formally apply Christian values to the life of the parish and maximally to show that the work of evangelization and catechesis is paramount in what the parish is about."

One priest, reflecting the consensus of his table partners, said that catechesis helps individuals become part of the community, and so is essential for individual development and the development of parish life. "It engages us to respond in our own words, to tell our own story with the story of the church, to give us a sense that we understand and we have the experiences to share." Catechesis "impacts the worship experience, enables people to take what is said and cherish it and make it part of their own experience and share that with their families or their communities." The group also viewed catechesis as an entry into greater participation in the parish. Once people become involved through catechesis, they frequently apply their energies to other ministries.

The reports illustrated several ways in which catechesis affects the entirety of parish life. Several participants explained that catechesis and evangelization provide the framework for the mission statement, which in turn establishes the goals and direction for the parish. Catechesis then continues to be used in the formation of the parish and of the ministers and ministries in the parish. As one priest stated, catechesis sustains all the activities of the parish, for without it "you don't have anything else."

As stated in the *General Catechetical Directory*: "It is necessary, therefore, that catechesis be associated with other pastoral activities, that is, with the biblical, liturgical, and ecumenical movements, with the lay apostolate and social action, and so on. Besides, it must be kept in mind that this cooperation is necessary from the very outset, that is, from the time the studies and plans for the organization of pastoral work are started." (*GCD*, 129)

Another group's report explained that catechesis entails a partnership among all the members and generations of the parish community—lay people and priests, adults and children, single people and families. Each contributes to the faith journey of the other. If people are to love Jesus, they must love all the members of the body of Christ and therefore become the body of Christ actively loving. Catechesis helps them achieve this.

The discussions highlighted several methods for the implementation of catechesis involving the entire community. People from one group commented that catechesis is not just an intellectual process. Rather, it is the faith developed, an integrated message of community and service. One of the participants stated that, in his parish, catechesis is part of the agenda of all meetings and societies. His parish's mission statement provides for this.

NOTES

Responses from the symposium participants

Informing the parish about catechetical responsibilities:

- The parish is asked to support and pray for the catechetical ministry and lay formation program. Everyone is also encouraged to participate or serve as a volunteer.

- The parish actively participates in recruiting catechists, commissioning the catechists, and affirming and supporting the catechists.

- On Catechetical Sunday the entire parish community is blessed and commissioned to emphasize the catechetical role of entire community.

- On Catechetical Sunday the catechists are presented and recognized.

- Ceremonies at Sunday Masses recognize various levels of attainment on the part of the young people who participate in programs.

- The catechists receive ongoing catechetical training and "in-service" throughout the year.

- The celebration of the sacraments of initiation and the rites of the RCIA are used to remind the assembly of its responsibility.

- Several parish homilies address the role of sharing faith.

- The announcements at liturgy highlight all the different forms of catechesis offered in the parish.

- The vision of the role of all members of the parish as catechists is shared in the "Pastor's letter" in the parish bulletin, in homilies, and in meetings with parish leadership groups. The DRE also emphasizes this vision in articles in the parish newsletter.

- Communication occurs through letters with the parents, posters, bulletin inserts, flyers from parish school of religion and school.

- Use time during Sunday sessions for parent gathering to pray scripture.

- Pre-Sacrament programs for parents take place after Sunday Mass as a visible sign for the worshiping community.

- Parents become aware of their catechetical responsibilities in our sacramental catechesis prior to Baptism, Reconciliation, First Eucharist and Confirmation.

- The parish stresses continued catechesis through adult sessions, prayer and Bible group and small group discussion.

- Cooperative efforts are made among neighboring parishes for updating, training, and certification of catechists.

- Inform parish of diocesan and parish sponsored workshops and events.

- The parish holds religious book sales after Masses two times each year.

- Report on the catechetical ministry of the parish to the Parish Assembly and Pastoral Council.

Once catechesis becomes an integral focus of the parish's mission, the mission statement becomes an important tool to implement catechesis. One report explained that the mission statement keeps the pastoral council and other groups in the parish focused. It serves as a standard to help them set goals and as a tool to evaluate progress in the light of their mission. Catechesis and dialogue lead to the mission statement, and reflection and evaluation lead back to catechesis. It is both a circular and dynamic process.

To establish and sustain this focus, one parish holds an annual meeting. Here the expectations of the parish are explicitly stated. Members of the staff present their plans for catechetics in the parish for the coming year, and they address their hopes and expectations for the involvement of the parishioners. Ideas from parishioners are solicited. What do they think of the plans? How can they participate? What will be their level of commitment? What other areas would they like to see covered?

Overall, participants related a number of things being done to help instill in the parish community a sense of responsibility for catechesis. A number of responses from the reflection questions appear on the opposite page. Several additional ideas surfaced during the meeting. For example, one parish has a community gathering on occasional Wednesday nights for fellowship and some instruction. Several pastors said they make sure that catechesis or religious education can take place on Sunday mornings without conflicting with liturgy or other activities. In order to bring the community to awareness, some pastors said they hire qualified, professional people involved in catechetical ministry, and try to model with their own staffs what the whole parish ought to be in terms of catechesis. And, of course, the homily plays a prominent role.

A participant observed that the role of catechesis as a ministry, and calling people into ministerial formation, is a key element that had added a new dimension to catechesis. Catechists now see themselves as ministers, not only helping in the work of the church, but making it their work. This outlook has had a broad effect. During the discussion a pastor observed that people who are actively involved in catechetical programs frequently develop a strong sense of ministry and become parish leaders. "Since catechesis/religious education is viewed as a formation process, it plays a key role in the life and mission of our parish. Leadership in all other ministries comes from an effective catechetical ministry and lay formation. It is through parish leadership that the parish's mission is more clearly articulated and carried out."

Another pastor stated that in his parish the people who are involved in intentional catechesis are also involved in social action programs and other parish ministries. They see catechesis as part of a much broader vision of the Church and ministry, and they recognize that the life of the parish requires many things. He thought it was pertinent that in the reflections on catechesis no one viewed catechesis as exclusively designed for children. The participants themselves have this broad vision of catechetical ministry.

<u>NOTES</u>

This observation contains a distinction made by some participants—intentional catechesis versus unintentional catechesis. One might refer to these terms more commonly as formal and informal. To them, what might be called formal catechesis includes programs designed for information, formation, and spiritual growth in which a person chooses to participate. Complementing this would be informal catechesis. As a participant said, it is the awareness that "each moment of liturgy, fellowship, social activity, community outreach, play, work, study and service is an opportunity to catechize through word and example."

A similar distinction is expressed in *Adult Catechesis in the Christian Community,* a document of the International Council for Catechesis. "Catechesis *per se* has to be *distinguished* therefore from other activities, even though it cannot be separated from them: it is different from evangelization, which is the proclamation of the Gospel for the first time to those who have not heard it, or the re-evangelization of those who have forgotten it; it is different from formal religious education, which goes beyond the basic elements of faith in more systematic and specialized courses; it is also different from those informal occasions for faith awareness in God's presence, which arise in fragmentary and incidental ways in the daily life of adults." (*Adult Catechesis in the Christian Community,* 32)

Finally, the participants noted that although some people are active catechists and parish leaders, obstacles still exist. As one person reported, a large portion of the parish budget is devoted to catechesis, but that does not mean that the whole community feels responsible for catechesis. The staff finds itself struggling to bring the community to that awareness.

Reflection

In what ways does your parish incorporate catechesis into its activities? How can this integration be improved or increased?

Adult Directed Catechesis

Hence, it is not only legitimate, but necessary, to acknowledge that a fully Christian community can exist only when a systematic catechesis of all its members takes place and when an effective and well-developed catechesis of adults is regarded as the <u>central</u> <u>task</u> in the catechetical enterprise.

Adult Catechesis in the Christian Community, 25

Woven throughout the reports were references regarding catechesis for adults. This outlook closely reflects the *National Catechetical Directory*, which states that the lives of adult Christians should exemplify gospel values to the young members of the Christian community and the rest of society. Therefore, "it is essential that they express gospel values by living with the hope and joy that come with faith. The Church, for its part, must encourage its adult members to grow in faith and give them opportunities to do so." (*NCD*, 40)

Referring to adult catechesis, a pastor recalled former modes of catechesis in identifying present and future needs. "When I was a kid we had presacramental catechesis—we didn't use those words perhaps, but CCD. All those structures are already in place and they are traditionally things that people are looking for in a parish. Our task is to shift the paradigm, insert the updated, to use the new language, to share the new vision in a structure that's already there."

Commenting on this, another pastor said that in addition to existing realities, there is a new dimension to catechesis. Not only are there opportunities to learn more, but these opportunities "are the means whereby we become ministers. The whole sense of ministry, the development of lay ministries as an integral part of the parish, calling more and more people into those ministries gives [catechesis] a whole new dimension that manifests itself in many, many other subconscious ways." He continued to say that "the whole development of the small group ministries gives people a sense that they become ministers and they're doing it as a result of their basic baptismal Christianity, and not because they are called to do so by the priest." Another priest echoed this: "The whole parish is the catechist via baptism. That is our function."

The participants spoke of programs for adult catechesis that use an adult to adult way to get adults talking about faith and where the Lord is in their lives. Areas mentioned include small faith communities, RENEW, and involvement in RCIA. *Adult Catechesis in the Christian Community* explains that adults must "actively participate in [the community's] various faith expressions and accept some form of responsibility for community life. For this reason, the building of *small communities or ecclesial groups* is conducive to the strengthening of adult catechesis. (*Catechesi Tradendae*, 24)" (*ACCC*, 69) One pastor stated his belief that an added benefit of small communities is that they reach out to those who do not join with the assembly for worship.

NOTES

Several other approaches to adult catechesis surfaced during the discussions. The role of sponsors in sacramental formation programs helps both the sponsored and the sponsor, involving the support of the community in this process. One parish has sponsor couples for marriage preparation as a way of deepening faith life and family life. Another parish offers unusual catechetical moments, such as a couple getting married at a Sunday Mass and reflecting on their own future life, thus giving witness to the sacrament of Matrimony. One pastor referred to his parish's baptismal seminars, saying: "The key [is] baptism, know who we are in baptism. Our baptismal seminars can help parishioners understand who they are and what their mission is in terms of their own role."

The *National Catechetical Directory* explains that the form adult catechesis takes will depend on a variety of factors, such as the size and makeup of the parish, and the cultural and educational background of the parishioners. "There are a number of appropriate models: small group discussions, lectures with questions and discussions, retreat programs, sacramental programs, dialogues between adults and young people, adult catechumenate." (*NCD*, 225)

Two impediments to adult catechesis were identified by the participants. The first may be defined as the historical philosophical viewpoint of a parish. One participant wrote that some adults in his parish do not view formation as a priority, that they "do not experience the church as addressing their life needs. Formation preference around life needs seems to offer the best possibility."

The design of the physical plant was identified as another potential obstacle. One participant referred to ". . . the architecture of our churches or buildings, which are either conducive or non-conducive for good catechesis." He said that in many Protestant churches, people can often walk into a complex and recognize the priority of education. However, Catholic parishes also address this need. As one pastor explained. "We built a new religious education parish center with ten meeting rooms. We have monthly formation sessions for our catechists. The coordinators form together the parish religious education committee. We want to expand our youth ministry and hire a part time youth ministry director."

It is not necessary to build a new wing for the parish plant, but it is necessary to offer adequate facilities for study and reflection. What does the parish budget to develop and maintain the worship space as compared to the space used for catechesis? A commensurate effort should be spent on creating an environment conducive to catechetical endeavors. Does the parish have rooms that are comfortable, well-lit, quiet, and free from distractions? As appropriate furnishings facilitate participation in liturgy, comfortable chairs, tables or desks facilitate catechesis. Catechesis and worship are synergistic, so the quality of the space designated for catechesis cannot be underestimated.

Catechesis in the Parish

NOTES

Reflection

What specific catechetical opportunities does your parish offer for adults? How is adult catechesis integrated into other parish programs?

What facilities in your parish are used for catechesis?

NOTES

Family as Primary Catechist

It rests with parents to prepare their children from an early age, within the family circle, to discern God's love for all men; they will teach them little by little—and above all by their example—to have concern for their neighbors' needs, material and spiritual. The whole family, accordingly, and its community life should become a kind of apprenticeship to the apostolate.   Decree on the Apostolate of Lay People, 30

The formational task is not limited solely to parenting. It is the responsibility of all members of the family to promote the development and potential of each member at every age.   A Family Perspective in Church and Society, page 20

The importance of beginning lifelong catechesis with children, incorporating family members and other members of the adult parish community in this catechesis, was evident from the catechetical efforts shared by the priests. Parishioners of all ages reap benefits from this catechetical interaction. In his Apostolic Exhortation *On Evangelization in the Modern World*, Pope Paul VI states: "The family, like the church, ought to be a place where the Gospel is transmitted and from which the Gospel radiates. In a family which is conscious of this mission, all the members evangelize and are evangelized. The parents not only communicate the Gospel to their children, but from their children they can themselves receive the same Gospel as deeply lived by them. And such a family becomes the evangelizer of many other families, and of the neighborhood of which it forms part." (*Evangelii Nuntiandi*, 71)

Pope John Paul II writes that "parents are through the witness of their lives the first heralds of the Gospel for their children." (*Familiaris Consortio*, 39) Pastors and catechists must encourage this faith formation within the family, as well as involve the children and their families in catechesis offered by the parish. Some parents may participate in adult catechesis, but the experience shared at the symposium was that many do not, and frequently may not be active parishioners. As one priest observed: "For many, religious education of a child is the first contact that some families have with the parish. It is through the catechetical program that many families are welcomed to the parish."

This presents both a challenge and an opportunity because "the success of programs for children and youth depends to a significant extent upon the words, attitudes, and actions of the adult community, especially parents, family and guardians." (*National Catechetical Directory*, 188) Catechesis may be needed to help parents rekindle a dormant faith, energize a complacent faith, or continue to enrich a faith that is fully open to development.

Though adult members of some families may not be involved actively in catechetics before their children enter catechetical programs, the experiences indicate that participation increases once the formal catechesis of the child begins. Reflecting on the evening's discussions, a participant observed: "I noticed from everyone, kind of, involvement of the whole family and the community in catechetics, whereas my experience years ago with catechetics was something that teachers did to children, and adults were left out of it. That's just a current I've seen through all the reports."

The reports also illustrated a family centered emphasis for faith sharing and catechesis that supports the continuing faith formation of adults. This occurs through a variety of methods, including community gatherings, neighborhood small faith communities, adult formation, and sacramental preparation. *The Challenge of Adolescent Catechesis* contains similar recommendations: "Acknowledging the importance of the family in catechesis means sponsoring programs for parents around their areas of need, creating parent catechetical experiences that parallel the adolescent catechetical program, sponsoring intergenerational catechetical experiences, and supporting parents in their catechetical ministry." (*CAC*, page 6) And as one pastor stated, priests can use homilies and liturgies to address the primary role of parents and guardians in the faith formation of their children, and to support the adults in this role.

Adult catechesis designed for parents in the parish of one of the participants includes marriage enrichment, programs to help them in the role of parenting, retreat days, and church updates. In addition, the parish tries to involve the entire family in the children's catechesis. For example, parents are often encouraged to attend and help in their children's catechetical sessions. In one instance, parents occasionally teach a weekly lesson while the regular catechist attends formation sessions.

Offering an example of expanded family involvement, a pastor explained that his state permits schools to release children for religious education. However, parishes moved away from released time because they found it was not the most effective approach for catechesis. According to the pastor, switching catechesis to Sunday, as many parishes have done, has helped increase the participation of parents. "There's much more parental involvement now than I'd say there was twenty years ago."

The comment about Sunday schedules reflects the attempt of parishes to make catechesis convenient for families with busy schedules. The parishes of many of the participants provide adult catechesis at the same time as for the children. This often may be on Sunday morning since this is time the family has earmarked for being together for liturgy. In one parish, when programs in the evenings are necessary for parents, baby-sitting and other types of support are given to families. The parish views baby-sitting as an important support to catechetical programs, especially for adults. The parish also offers baby-sitting during Sunday liturgies so that parents will not have to worship separately while one or the other stays at home with the small children.

NOTES

NOTES

Catechesis in the Parish

Reflection

In your parish, how do adult family members regard their role in the catechesis of children? What can be done to further encourage family participation?

Implementation of Catechesis

Several examples and suggestions for encouraging the involvement of families in catechesis were offered. During one report, a participant spoke of setting up opportunities for families to share faith. This may take the form of discussions as a family after church on Sunday about the homily and the Sunday celebration, or it may be lectionary based sharing in which families prepare and discuss the Sunday readings.

Other examples include alternative programs that offer a family cluster in catechesis, and training catechists to help parents catechize, rather than having the catechists teach the children. Family activities and prayer service resources are sent home, and children receive assignments that require the input of family members. Further support includes offering parents practical activities, such as bulletins or videos, that can be used at home during the liturgical year. One participant explained that his parish chooses catechetical materials for school and parish programs that have a strong focus on family involvement. "We see a partnership between family and church in the role of handing on the principles and traditions of our Catholic faith."

Another area of adult involvement was sacramental preparation. One pastor explained that his parish has First Penance and First Eucharist preparation conducted by and for parents. Parents from one year's group work with the next year's group. Also in this parish at least one adult joins each young person at Confirmation sessions, and some young people have two or three adults accompanying them. The pastor, of course, is available to the parents' groups.

The pastor described the effect the parish's catechetical program had on the formation of the young people. Young people from the sixth grade to senior year in high school presume they will be altar servers, greeters, or lectors according to their gifts and abilities. They also presume they will participate in service projects on a regular basis, and not only as a Confirmation prerequisite. Parishioners voluntarily take youth's service project forms and supervise one, two, or as many young people as they can, calling them each month. The pastor said the programs almost take care of themselves.

The Challenge of Adolescent Catechesis notes: "Effective catechesis with youth requires that the adult members of our community grow continually in their faith and in their ability to share it with others. This growth is especially necessary for the parents of adolescents. We cannot expect more of youth than we do of adults. The ways we adults learn about, express, and live out faith is a vigorous support or a serious obstacle in effectively catechizing youth. (*Challenge of Adolescent Catechesis*, page 3)

An interesting activity was related by a pastor with a parish of three hundred families. "During Lent I visit as many homes as I can. I ask for the whole family to be there, or as many as possible, for two hours. (If there's a meal, three hours.) We do faith sharing and try to see how the upcoming Sunday gospel relates to life. We hope to touch parents so that they can share their faith, and young people the same, that they "know" the faith." Discussions may involve church teachings and practices.

Finally, some pastors noted their parish staffs include the position of Family Minister. As one participant explained, this person helps to involve families in sacrament preparation and future family catechesis, which may entail parenting, formation in sexuality, and family prayer days.

Sacramental Formation

The participants spoke of the personal involvement of all parents in the sacramental formation of their children. For example, a pastor referred to personal interviews staff members hold with the parents to help them with this formation. As he explained: "We place a special emphasis on families being the prime educators of the faith as their children prepare for various sacraments." The activities he mentioned were workshops, take-home packets and projects "that invite parents and child to share their faith, beliefs, questions and attempts to live what they believe."

NOTES

Several other examples were offered. Most participants referred to parent catechesis for baptism. One pastor said that his parish has baptismal catechesis for all new parents which emphasizes the role of the parents as the primary influence on the religious development of their children. Another parish requires seven meetings with the parents and godparents, and some participants referred to baptism during the Sunday liturgy.

For Confirmation, one person stated that in his parish there are individual staff interviews with the young people seeking Confirmation. During these meetings the staff members explain the responsibilities and commitment of this sacrament and they discuss the expectations of the parish. Other pastors spoke of sponsor programs.

Some parishes have "enrollment celebrations" at the Sunday liturgy for all children preparing for First Eucharist, and others involve families in planning celebrations and liturgies with children. One priest wrote that his parish tries to develop an experience of family catechesis with First Eucharist families to empower parents to actually share faith experience with children. This has been designed to be a training module for future family experience.

Parochial Schools

Twelve of the pastors were responsible for parochial schools, and one of them also has a high school in the parish. As the *National Catechetical Directory* explains, it is an integrated challenge. "A parochial school is also a community within the wider community, contributing to the parish upon which it depends and integrated into its life. Integration and interdependence are major matters of parish concern; each program in a total catechetical effort should complement the others." (*NCD*, 232) This point is also emphasized in a later document, *The Religious Dimension of Education in a Catholic School*. "Religious instruction in the school needs to be coordinated with the catechesis offered in parishes, in the family, and in youth organizations." (*Religious Dimension of Education*, 70)

One of the pastors reflected on the catechetical challenges involved in a parish that has a school. "In our parish, the whole parish mission is centered around catechetics; we have the traditional method of catechesis for all ages and we have, even, an adult catechesis similar to the RENEW program. However, the greatest effort surrounds grammar and high school religious education programs. Within the Catholic School we would like to see some program directed to the parents of the students to see if we could motivate them to a better attendance at the Eucharist and a deeper commitment to the practice of their faith." Another priest explained that catechesis is a top priority in the parish school. Every teacher in the religion department has a Master's Degree in Theology, and students know that religion is a serious subject in the curriculum. As one person explained, "It is our direct contact with children, the next generation of Catholics."

Reflection

It is important also that the catechesis of children and young people, permanent catechesis, and the catechesis of adults should not be separate watertight compartments. It is even more important that there should be no break between them. On the contrary, their perfect complementarity must be fostered: adults have much to give to young people and children in the field of catechesis, but they can also receive much from them for the growth of their own Christian lives.

Catechesi Tradendae, 45

How does your parish foster lifelong and complementary catechesis for all parish members?

NOTES

Summary

The symposium's initial discussions illustrated parishes that display a strong sense of stewardship and entrust people with a sense of discipleship. The discussions covering "Catechesis in the Parish" displayed how these attributes are woven into catechesis. All members of the church community are called to develop and strengthen their loving relationship with God throughout their lifetime, and they are called to help others do the same.

The following comment, made by a participant to summarize a discussion, helps illustrate this point. "I think here we may be putting our finger on the key issue of this whole symposium. I think there is a real angst about the importance, the priority that needs to be given to catechesis in parish life. We used terms like: 'It's foundational to all other ministries;' 'You don't have it, you just don't have anything else;' 'That it's sustaining of the other ministries.' . . . There's a priority in terms of the way in which faith is developed, and if you don't have the ministry of the word, the others don't really happen very well."

These key points emerged from the participants during their discussions:

- Catechesis is faith formation and development.
- Catechesis is an ongoing development of faith that occurs from cradle to tomb. The foundation is rooted in family and childhood, but catechesis continues through adolescence and into adulthood. Being capable of a mature faith, adults have the responsibility for continuous spiritual growth.
- Catechesis begins and continues in the home, supported and complemented by parish programs for all age levels.
- Catechesis is intergenerationally supportive. All people within the family, and within the parish, can aid the faith formation of the other members—children, youth, adults, and the elderly.
- The ministry of the word is essential to a strong faith. Homilies must be prepared carefully and appropriate to the faithful.
- Catechesis is woven into all parish activities.

In short, the participants do not regard catechesis as a separate component that occurs on Sunday mornings between liturgies, on Tuesday afternoons after school, or on Thursday evenings after work. The ongoing development and discernment of faith takes place in all activities and responsibility falls on all members of the parish to catechize and evangelize.

The Next Step

What role does the priest play in catechesis in the parish? The next section will examine this important question.

Review your notes, reflections and discussions to the reflection questions for this chapter. In order to process this information, take some time to answer the questions on the next two pages. Your responses can also be used to help you complete the planning segment in Chapter 6.

☐☐ Planning Notes
■■ **Catechesis in the Parish**

Identify the catechetical activities and the opportunities for catechesis that occur in your parish. What are the strongest areas?

After reading the section, think of catechesis in your parish. What would you maintain? What might need to be adjusted?

What are some ways of strengthening existing programs?

What are some resources for change—people, material, programs?

Are there some obstacles to change? If so, how can your parish overcome them?

Chapter 3
The Priest in Catechetical Ministry

Introduction

Catechesis always has been and always will be a work for which the whole Church must feel responsible and must wish to be responsible. But the Church's members have different responsibilities, derived from each one's mission.

Catechesi Tradendae, 16

"How do you see yourselves in catechetical ministry?" This question began this segment of the symposium and remained the focal point for discussion as the participants considered the many possible responses. After examining the activities of the parish and how catechesis fits within the context of parish life, the participants transitioned to the role that the priest plays in catechetical ministry.

The *National Catechetical Directory* explains that "priests exercise a uniquely important role and have a special responsibility for the success of the catechetical ministry. They are a source of leadership, cooperation, and support for all involved in this ministry. As leaders in developing a faith community under the guidance of the Holy Spirit, they perform indispensable catechetical functions: encouraging catechists, praying with them, teaching and learning with them, supporting them." (*NCD*, 217) Regarding the role of the pastor, Canon 773 states: "There is a proper and serious duty, especially on the part of pastors of souls, to provide for the catechesis of the Christian people so that the faith of the faithful becomes living, explicit and productive through formation in doctrine and the experience of Christian living." (*Code of Canon Law*, 773)

The *Directory for the Life and Ministry of Priests* also refers to the mandate and responsibility that priests receive to encourage, coordinate and direct the catechetical activity of the community. It explains that a priest "must know how to integrate such activity into an organic project of evangelization, guaranteeing, above all, the communion of the catechesis of his community with the person of the Bishop, with the particular Church and with the universal Church." (*Ministry of Priests*, 47)

As discussed in Chapters 1 and 2, catechesis should not be limited to the classroom or specific programs, but should be incorporated into the entire fabric of parish life. Pope John Paul II writes that "the definitive aim of catechesis is to put people not only in touch but in communion, in intimacy, with Jesus Christ: only He can lead us to the love of the Father in the Spirit and make us share in the life of the Holy Trinity." (*Catechesi Tradendae*, 5) How do priests facilitate and encourage this communion with Jesus?

NOTES

NOTES

When asked about the role of priests in catechetical ministry, some people may picture the priest teaching in parish programs or in Catholic schools. Others may consider his involvement in the Rite of Christian Initiation of Adults, catechist training, or programs for adults. However, such programs and teaching opportunities cannot define or limit the role of priests in catechetical ministry.

Synopsis

This chapter examines many of the ways the participants and their colleagues participate in the catechetical ministry of their parishes. The symposium's exploration of the role of the priest in catechetical ministry utilized several interesting activities to explore the topic. At the end of the previous session, the participants each received blank paper and crayons and were asked to create an image that for them captures the role of priest in catechetical ministry. With the help of these visual presentations, table groups first compared and explained their drawings, and then created a single group image or a collage of images. These group efforts then were shared with the entire body. This exercise facilitated an informed examination of the role of the priest in catechetical ministry, and precipitated a discussion about the challenges of this role.

The participants next analyzed both the time they devote to parish activities and the time they spend in specific catechetical activities. The exercise was designed to help the participants identify patterns present in this dimension of their ministry, and the evaluation served as the foundation for a free-flowing, revolving interplay of thoughts, ideas, and reactions.

As in the previous chapters, you will have the opportunity to complete the same exercises to help you reflect on you own experience and compare it with the experience of the symposium's participants.

Reflection Questions

In preparation for this section, please spend some time completing the reflection questions on the next three pages. As you read this chapter, continue to consider the responses from the symposium as benchmarks for comparison with your responses. Engage in a mental dialogue.

Some responses from the reflection questions of the participants describing the role of the priest in parish catechetical ministry appear after the questions and throughout the chapter.

■□ Reflection Questions
■■ **The Priest in Catechetical Ministry**

How do you personally influence the parish's catechetical ministry?

How do you and the parish DRE/Coordinator of Religious Education support each other?

How do you help prepare catechists for their role in this ministry?

■□ Reflection Questions
■■ **The Priest in Catechetical Ministry** (Continued)

Name the three most important priorities for the parish catechetical ministry.

Describe your personal continuing education in the area of catechesis/religious education:

- What specific steps do you take?

- How do you utilize diocesan services and resources?

- Why do you pursue this continuing education?

- What are the obstacles to this pursuit?

Reflection Questions
The Priest in Catechetical Ministry (Continued)

Based on your experience, what important points would you make to impart your vision of catechesis/religious education in the life of the parish, if you were speaking with:

- A newly hired DRE?

- A new catechist?

- A newly ordained priest?

■□ Reflection Questions
■■ **The Priest in Catechetical Ministry** (Continued)

How would you describe the role of the pastor/priest in parish catechesis/religious education to:

- A newly hired DRE?

- A new catechist?

- A newly ordained priest?

Responses from the symposium participants

Describe the role of the pastor and priest in parish catechesis:

- Works with the DRE and other catechetical leaders in collaboration, keeping in mind that the administration of the program is primarily their responsibility.
- Ministers to the ministers. Is present to the catechists as an ongoing affirmation of their importance in the parish's work.
- Articulates a vision of the whole parish as catechist and evangelist.
- Enables people to recognize their gifts, provides the opportunities for them to develop their gifts, and motivates them to share their gifts. One of these gifts is the gift of their faith and their personal faith story.
- Preaches well and with enthusiasm.
- Is of service, answers questions but does not interfere. The gift of faith resides among all the parishioners, not just the pastor. It is the faith that we are called to share.
- Focuses the parish's mission on the Gospel and God's self-revelation.

How do you help prepare catechists?

- By assisting in formation, in-service, and retreats, and by sending several of the experienced catechists to be trained as master catechists, who in turn offer ongoing training to the catechists.
- Well-trained people coordinate our programs, providing the materials, training, vision, and organization for a well-run program. They conduct ongoing assessment and evaluation.
- The DRE and Coordinators give monthly ongoing formation sessions for catechists, and there are training and formation sessions at the end of the summer and the beginning of September.
- By working with a full time Pastoral Associate for religious education and a full time Pastoral Associate for youth ministry. My personal involvement in catechist preparation comes through various seminars and workshops.
- Hiring and supporting a gifted DRE who does most of the hands-on preparation, and letting catechists know I see their work as ministry.
- By assisting the staff in this work as requested and being available to support and assist catechists on request.
- Working with the DRE, Principal, and Pastoral Associate, we identify needs of those who will be working as catechists. We talk with our volunteers and determine their needs, concerns, and areas of interest. We then offer mini-workshops or updating on those areas. We also connect our catechists with area workshops and certification programs.
- By participating in meetings and prayer services, and by seeking out candidates to serve as catechists, encouraging them to come forth.

NOTES

The Role of the Priest in Catechetical Ministry, Artfully Rendered

When the participants were asked to draw an image that captured for them the role of the priest in catechetical ministry, people were somewhat curious about the artistic and catechetical outcomes. The denouement turned out to be enlightening, filled with images that were at times insightful, at times humorous, and at all times creative.

A proverb explains that a picture is worth a thousand words. However, in this case the descriptions are more powerful than the images. Objects as diverse as a stagecoach, a fireball, an oil can, and a cartoon character, as well as some fairly abstract images, were cleverly used and expressively explained. During one presentation a priest commented: "It's very good theology, very poor art."

These images and their descriptions will be reviewed. But before you continue, the next page was left blank for you to create *your* image of the priest in catechetical ministry. Find some crayons, colored pencils or markers. You can use a pen or pencil, but color always gives added dimension. Have some fun, be creative. Let your "right brain" go to work as you create your image of the priest in catechetical ministry.

NOTES

Images

The drawings created by the participants contain images and symbols that offer interesting insights into the role of the priest in catechetical ministry. Since the objective of this exercise was to facilitate an examination of this role, this section reviews the themes that emerged from the images rather than descriptions and explanations of the images themselves. The themes include:

- Priest as Empowerer
- Common Thread
- Priest as Leader
- Tightrope Walker

Priest as Empowerer

The discussions to this point in the symposium reflected a commitment on the part of the participants to help all the baptized recognize their roles and responsibilities as part of the Church community, and also to help them be open to the power of the Spirit. Pope John Paul II referred to this responsibility in his Apostolic Exhortation *The Vocation and the Mission of the Lay Faithful in the Church and in the World*: "The lay faithful, precisely because they are members of the Church, have the vocation and mission of proclaiming the Gospel: They are prepared for this work by the sacraments of Christian initiation and by the gifts of the Holy Spirit." (*Christifideles Laici*, 33) The sense of mission must be nurtured.

The *Dogmatic Constitution on the Church* speaks of the fruits of this relationship. "Many benefits for the Church are to be expected from this familiar relationship between the laity and the pastors. The sense of their own responsibility is strengthened in the laity, their zeal is encouraged, they are more ready to unite their energies to the work of their pastors. The latter, helped by the experience of the laity, are in a position to judge more clearly and more appropriately in spiritual as well as in temporal matters." (*Lumen Gentium*, 37)

Several pictures and their descriptions captured the concept of an empowering relationship between the priest and the parishioners. For example:

- The light on Holy Saturday from the fire started by the priest and passed by members of the community to one another. The light shines in the community because people who have been touched by the light become light and carry the light to others.

- A fireball in the universe. This image represents the priest as an energizing minister who helps the faithful realize their potential as ministers in the parish's journey of faith. In the midst of this journey, the priest and parishioners work together and energize one another to reach their common goal of new life in the parish.

- A priest laying hands on the community, representing the efforts to bring forth the wonderful gifts of each person in the community to serve the ministry of catechesis.

- A watch, with the priest as a battery that provides power to start the mechanism moving. With interconnected gears, the priest moves certain people who in a sense move everything else. There is community, yet individuality.

One priest described an intricate image to illustrate the empowering image of the priest in catechetical ministry. The image had eight wings emanating from a center point, which symbolized Christ. The design reflected the premise of mutuality—all are created in the image and likeness of God. He explained: "We are all meant to soar. As the priest lifts his wings to soar he also lifts up all others and they lift him. Lifting one wing requires lifting everyone else. Each wing has an opposing wing which symbolizes our shadow. As we call forth each other's gifts we must also develop and call forth the shadow side lest we are not whole. It is only when all are whole that we are balanced and our flight is harmonious and we live in the Hebrew concept of Shalom. Our flight now spirals upward ever more deeply into the mystery of God."

Priest as Leader, Working with Others

Several participants illustrated the priest as a catechetical leader who has and shares a vision, which is implemented in a way that involves all of the talents and abilities of everyone. This recalls the first letter of Paul to the Thessalonians. "Be at peace among yourselves. Do not quench the Spirit. Do not despise prophetic utterances. Test everything; retain what is good." (1 Thessalonians 5:13, 19–21)

However, in his Apostolic Exhortation Pope John Paul II cautions that no charism dispenses a person from reference and submission to the pastors of the church. He writes: "The Council clearly states: 'Judgment as to their (charisms) genuineness and proper use belongs to those who preside over the Church, and to whose special competence it belongs, not indeed to extinguish the Spirit, but to test all things and hold fast to what is good (cf. 1 Thessalonians 5:12, 19–21),' (*Lumen Gentium*, 12) so that all the charisms might work together, in their diversity and complementarity, for the common good. (cf. *Lumen Gentium*, 30)" (*Christifideles Laici*, 24)

The following descriptions of the images depict women, men, and priests working together in their parishes for this common goal.

- A flower, with parishioners as its beautiful petals and the pastor in the center. The pastor has contact and interrelationships with parishioners, respects the boundaries and the role of leadership of others, and provides a source of unification. Everyone is interconnected through the work, sharing, and vision.
- A stagecoach. The priest helps to direct everyone's energy – with good ideas and bad ideas, and then keeps all working together and moving in the same direction.
- The pastor as a light that exemplifies where catechesis should be leading people.
- The pastor as salt that energizes, preserves tradition, and gives taste.
- Another group offered a drawing of a priest with exaggerated features: big ears—he's a good listener; a big smile; big eyes—to see a lot; and a big heart to engage people in relationship, example, support, belief, trust, and encouragement.

NOTES

- The people at one table opted not to share a drawing, but instead offered their images by means of "performance art" in which each person at the table stood, and explained how the fluid motion of the wrist illustrates a feature of the priest's catechetical ministry:

    - It is all in the wrist, hands that enable, hands that receive, hands that give. It is a shared responsibility among people to form, inform, and transform a community in Christian faith.
    - The priest striking the match and inviting everybody else to strike their match and let the flame come alive.
    - The conductor leading an orchestra in which all people have gifts. They do things differently, but they come together through the leader and the wrist in harmony and melodic unity.
    - Like the mechanism for a movable, geometric shape, the priest in catechesis can twist and turn on a variety of axes, but hold things together and eventually help things turn out right, though right does not mean identical.

Common Thread

One group assembled a collage by taping their six drawings to a flipchart and then connecting those drawings with yarn sewn through the paper. The spokesperson for the group explained that the image of weaving represents the ability of parishes to maintain several images together at many different moments in the ebb and flow of parish life and activity. The group felt that any one image, though it may be an excellent one, is not always applicable. When the images are woven together, there will probably be a very dynamic community of faith.

The Vocation and the Mission of the Lay Faithful states: "All the members of the People of God—clergy, men and women religious, the lay faithful—are laborers in the vineyard. At one and the same time they all are the goal and subjects of Church communion as well as of participation in the mission of salvation. Every one of us possessing charisms and ministries, diverse yet complementary, works in the one and the same vineyard of the Lord." (*Christifideles Laici*, 55)

The Tightrope Walker

One group offered a different type of picture. It illustrated a priest on a tightrope juggling several items. Behind the priest on the tightrope stands a person ready to challenge him whenever the two disagree about the purpose or outcome of activities, especially those that the priest thinks are great, but the other person does not. All the while the priest continues to juggle many things, although some are dropped and end up broken. However, through all this the priest keeps walking towards a goal.

Reflection

Describe your illustration of the priest in catechetical ministry to a friend or colleague. Solicit a response.

Realistic Appraisals

Pastoral ministry is a fascinating undertaking, yet arduous, open to misunderstanding and marginalisation, and, especially today, to fatigue, challenge, isolation and, at times, solitude. Directory for the Life and Ministry of Priests, 37

With the exception of the tightrope walker, all the pictures and their descriptions conveyed positive images and optimistic outlooks. However, an image that energizes one person could raise warning flags for someone else, and although it is good to be energized, realism must also be considered. Thus, the participants were offered the opportunity to raise concerns about the roles just discussed. This invitation drew many observations.

Excessive Expectations

Immediately, one priest cautioned against "putting too great an expectation on ourselves." Another pastor agreed, saying he was most threatened by that same sense of excessive expectations. "I'm supposed to be the light and the salt, and I'm supposed to be the connector, and I'm supposed to be the center. . . . I wake up in the morning and I'm not. I need to have a safe place where I can just be me without all the stuff. Just be the weak person who has no more or no less gifts than anybody else, but working in a community that loves me and supports me and forgives me and protects me, and look to somebody else in the community to be, sometimes, that light and that center and that connectedness."

Referring to these expectations, as well as to the overall responsibilities of the pastor, one person told the group that he thinks the pastor has the hardest job in the Church. "Before Vatican II the pastor had a number of responsibilities. He had to maintain the plant. He had to make sure Masses were scheduled. You had to make sure that money was available, etc. And you did it all. You didn't have a staff. Staff meetings were called 'supper at the rectory' because that's where you saw all the associates."

He continued to observe that after Vatican II, none of those duties was taken away, and many were added. Pastors now must work with Parish Pastoral Councils, Finance Councils, and Liturgy Committees. They now must supervise a staff, with attendant contracts and staff meetings. There are also now diocesan responsibilities, such as long range planning committees. "So I'm not aware that we took away anything, but we've added an awful lot to the role of pastor."

Concurring with this position, a pastor said that for many priests today, one of the most significant challenges can be expressed as: "Can I be myself and meet the expectations I'm finding?" As a follow-up, another pastor explained that in many dioceses priests do not want to become pastors because of these responsibilities and expectations. He believes that one of the challenges that pastors face is to approach catechetical ministry in such a way that goals are achieved without the person being overwhelmed. "I think perhaps one of the challenges we have in our role in the area supporting catechetics is to handle it in a way that you don't have to be a superman to make it happen."

NOTES

The Role of Lay People

After having described Christian formation as "a continual process in the individual of maturation in faith and a likening to Christ, according to the will of the Father, under the guidance of the Holy Spirit," they [the 1987 world Synod of Bishops] have clearly affirmed that the formation of the lay faithful must be placed among the priorities of a diocese. It ought to be so placed within the plan of pastoral action that the efforts of the whole community (clergy, lay faithful, and religious) converge on this goal. (Proposition 40)

Christifideles Laici, 57

Responding to the initial observation about responsibilities since the Second Vatican Council, a priest suggested that the church gave everyone a theology of ecclesiology and widespread sense of ministry, but did not train people sufficiently for the skills to function in that mode. Therefore, many people have "the language without the skills."

Another pastor suggested that an answer for the problems caused by these expectations might be to implement a different model of the Church. This person stated that the pastoral team must begin to share the responsibility that the individual pastor once had exclusively. "Most of us can't play all the roles because we come from who we are. Some of us are energizers, some of us are relational people, other people are administrators, other people bring people together, other people just are action. But I don't think I can be, or anybody can be, all of it. I think many people in the parish I serve have said: 'You can't be everything.' I think that's difficult for us to accept, but it suggests that there is a different model."

Another pastor also spoke of the need to develop lay ministry. He said the models being discussed call for a concerted effort for this development on the part of both dioceses and parishes. In this way the pastor and people can develop a vision and work together to accomplish it. This development will enhance the catechetical efforts of the parish because it will facilitate the use of more gifts and talents.

An observation from someone in a parish with more than two thousand families suggested that often lay people who want training and responsibility do not, as one might reasonably expect, lessen the expectations that they place upon the priest. In his situation, the parish currently has five times as many families as it did thirty years ago, but it now has a developed lay ministry. However, many people still expect the pastor to visit all the parishioners, just as the pastor did when there were only a few hundred people. It presents a conflict in terms of expectations.

Another comment focused on the contrast of the idealized vision of the priest possessed by some lay people versus the practical reality being expressed by the participants. Referring back to one of the drawings that was presented, the person suggested that lay people may need to put a safety net under the priest who is on the tightrope. However, some lay people may not know or understand how to do that, and so input from the pastor about what they could do would benefit everyone.

Differing Visions

A challenge also comes from differing visions of the Church. A participant explained that the pastors at the symposium may find the discussions about catechesis energizing and exciting, but this may not be the reality for the parish community. There are other visions of the Church that use a different set of images, and these differing ecclesiologies are present not only in the church on a national level, but also within the parish. When the pastor attempts to be the juggler, not only with these images of catechesis but with other expectations of the community he serves, the situation can become complicated. Even though pastors may find the concepts being discussed exciting, the ideas may not be as easy to implement.

Another participant empathized with these thoughts. He reflected that it is especially challenging for a pastor if parishioners come to liturgy with an expectation that seems to minimize the impact of the Second Vatican Council. The challenge increases if some people in diocesan leadership appear to be more sympathetic to these parishioners rather than with what the pastor may be doing in the ministry of the parish.

Role of the Word

For since nobody can be saved who has not first believed, it is the first task of priests as co-workers of the bishops to preach the Gospel of God to all men. In this way they carry out the Lord's command "Go into all the world and preach the Gospel to every creature" (Mark 16:15) and thus set up and increase the People of God.

Presbyterorum Ordinis, 4

Two pastors, commenting on the demands made on them, expressed their belief that the priority in the life of the priest should be proclaiming the gospel message. The first one stated: "I have a hunch that we are going to have to be more selective about what we are going to take on as pastors. And maybe we can be guided by the documents of the Church. I am thinking particularly about the document on priesthood which said that the 'premium officium' of the priest is to preach the word of God. I don't mean to take that in the narrow sense of just giving homilies or sermons. Maybe we have to reclaim and say that our particular role is that of prophet, the one who speaks for God. . . . Which means you probably need more time in prayer. I think part of the problem is that we are not claiming what is central to our priesthood and getting into all this other stuff. . . . Our central role is that of the word."

A second pastor continued this thought. "If you were to ask any Baptist what is the primary responsibility of their pastor, they'd tell you in a minute: 'Preach the word.' They've got other staff people who are responsible for all the other stuff, and so they can remain focused. I really think [he] is on to something there. We are so scattered in our focus, that burnout is such a problem for us that it would be clearer for us to measure our effectiveness if we were more focused. It's a real problem."

NOTES

> *Responses from the symposium participants*
>
> **What points would you make to impart your vision of catechesis in the life of the parish to a newly ordained priest?**
>
> - Keep learning, studying and discussing with others how to make your faith alive for people. Never pretend that you have all the answers. Take people and their needs seriously. Parishioners today are highly educated, ask deep rooted questions about life, faith, God, and religion as they try to make sense out of a complicated world. Trust their faith journey.
>
> - Meet with and learn from our DRE's.
>
> - Religious instruction without spirituality is, I believe, like a body without life, a romance without passion. We must find a way to bring the best of our Catholic tradition of spirituality to our people, young and old.
>
> - The center of parish is life of discipleship in community.
>   Catechesis helps the parishioner be aware of these dimensions of life.
>   Catechesis is done by the whole parish—the experience of belonging to a community of word, worship, service.
>   Catechesis happens, therefore, in more than classrooms.
>   Catechesis happens for all ages. The real challenge is to invite experience to be intergenerational.
>   Create opportunities for outreach and welcoming.
>
> - Parents are the first and foremost educators and it is our responsibility to enable them to do what they do best. Never lose sight of that fact. Be willing to take a lot of flack when you keep reminding them of their responsibility.
>
> - Work to build skills in collaboration and support. Know that you don't know it all and can't do it all! Use your best gifts to share the faith. Be available. Develop listening skills. Develop empowerment and delegating skills. Learn discerning skills.
>
> - The task of preaching to the people served is critical. People are looking for some handles to help them grapple with the question, "What is God doing in my life?" Preaching can help them see how God works in their lives.
>
> - Every very newly ordained priest should have responsibility for a couple of classes for a whole year or more to learn from experience the challenges of teaching, especially in a catechetical program.
>
> - Constantly invite parishioners to be part of programs, to share their lived experiences with others, to actively share their talents. Don't force people into "the open slot in the parish" if that is not their area of interest or expertise. Treat adults as adults and invite them to keep growing in their faith. Be a person of prayer, knowing that God is working with you, walking with you.
>
> - The family is smallest cell of the Church. Get to know families. You don't have to have all the answers—just listen, be there, and support them as they discover their answers.
>
> - Keep on reading. Listen attentively. Pray and learn with a group.

Reflection

How does your image of the priest in catechetical ministry compare with the ones expressed at the symposium? Are the challenges similar or different? How are the challenges addressed?

NOTES

Time Allocation for Catechesis

The first part of this symposium segment drew views from the pastors, both visual and verbal, about their role in catechesis and surfaced challenges as well as benefits.

The next exercise helped the participants examine their activities as effective catechists to see if there are identifiable common patterns. The exercise began with a simple analysis of time spent in general parish activities and then of time devoted specifically to catechesis. Each participant received two pages with empty circles and was asked to convert each circle into a pie chart, giving a general delineation of time spent on activities in the parish and in catechesis. For example, parish activities may include homily preparation, staff supervision, and visiting the sick. Catechesis may entail catechist training, RCIA, and meetings with the DRE or coordinator. As explained to the participants, these activities are not what is hoped for or planned, these are what actually occur.

Before continuing, please take some time to complete your own pie charts on the next two pages. Remember, the charts are not to record your hopes or plans for the future. They are to help you identify what you actually do today.

All that I do in the parish:

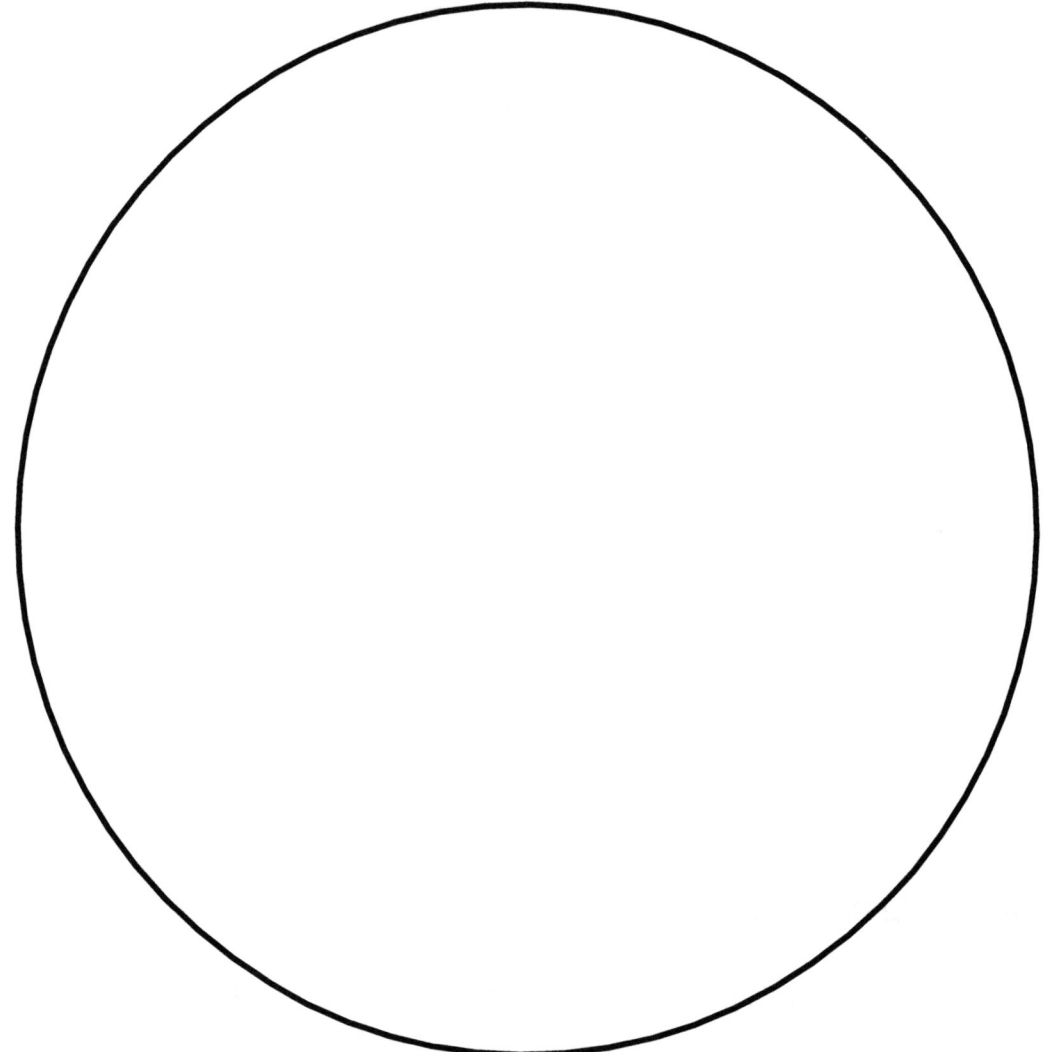

Notes:

All that I do in catechesis:

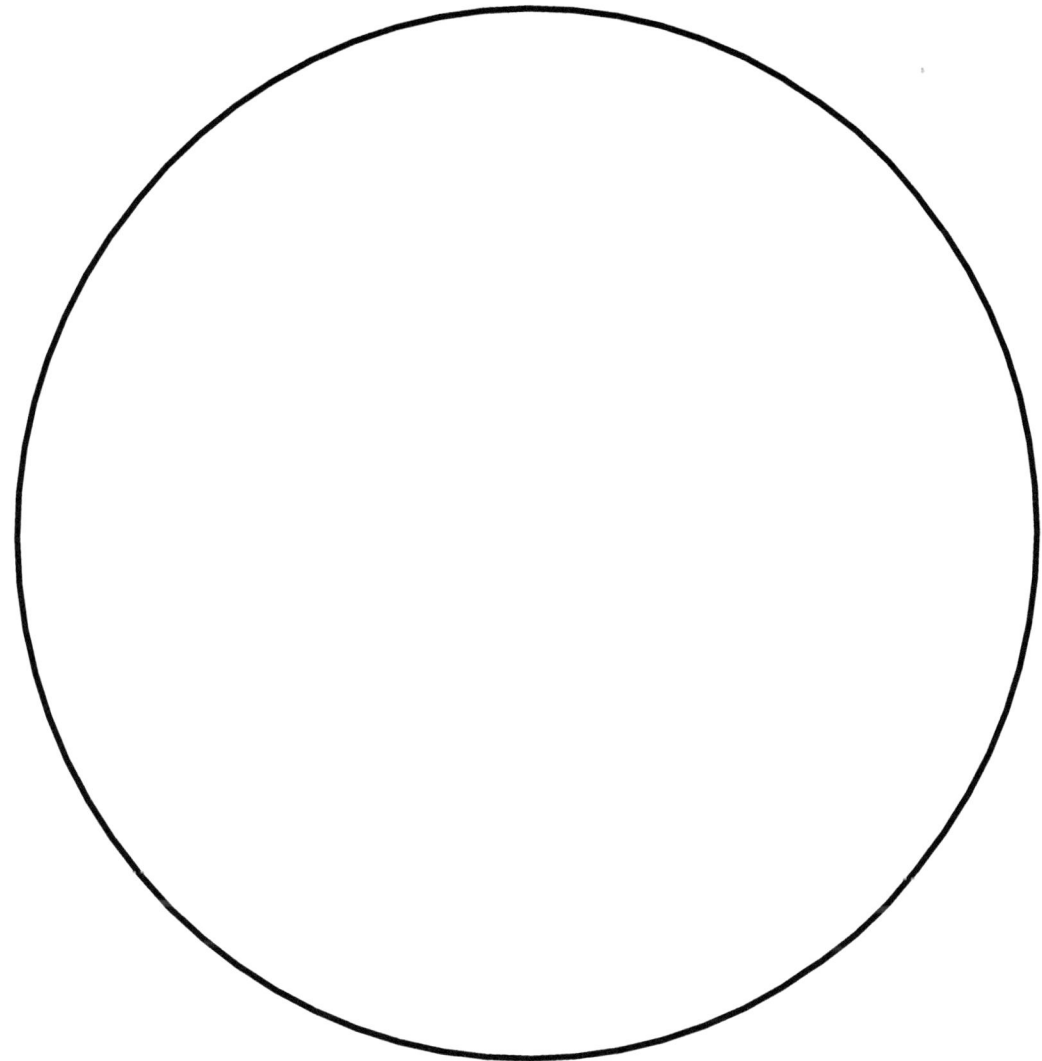

Notes:

NOTES

Analysis

After completing their initial analysis, the participants discussed their insights with the others at their table, sharing not only concrete actions performed, but also the attitude or feelings behind the actions. These observations were then shared with the rest of the group through a "fishbowl" exercise.

For this exercise eight chairs—one for each table plus two—were placed in a circle in the middle of the room. Each table initially sent one delegate to the fishbowl to report the gist of the discussion. To be part of any dialogue, a person had to occupy one of the chairs in the fishbowl circle, even if this was to comment on what was said or to offer additional remarks. When finished, the person left the circle, giving someone else an opportunity to join the circle and speak.

The presentation of this information does not connote an order of importance. As you read this section, become part of this interaction. How do you react to what is being said? What would you like to add?

Being Present to People

In recent years, in effect, it has become evident that there is an eminently pastoral necessity for the priest to be a man of God and a teacher of prayer. At the same time, this obliges the priest to be welcoming towards the community entrusted to his pastoral care in such a way that no member of the community would be made to feel anonymous or think themselves an object of indifference.

Directory for the Life and Ministry of Priests, 36

The exercise began as a spokesperson explained that he recognized a few patterns during the discussions at his table. One was the importance of presence. For example, priests must have an active presence and interest wherever catechesis occurs, whether for children or youths or adults or elderly. The second was the element of listening. It is important to be attentive to the stories people tell—stories of the gospel, stories of lives, stories of the Church in the world. The third was openness. Priests need to share their own stories, because teaching includes the sharing of stories.

Another pastor explained that the priests in his group also noted that they spend a good deal of time and energy interacting one on one with people. "Talking and listening, listening and talking. Sharing the story of life, sharing the story of Christianity. . . . One pastor [said] that the majority of his day was spent with individual appointments with people. And that becomes the catechetical interface, as it were. And it also becomes the stuff from which the catechetical pastor draws his preaching, his teaching, his catechizing."

A third person added that he identified telephone ministry as a role in catechesis. "A lot of things happen over the phone. Once you answer the phone it's an initiation to a one on one relationship." As he explained, it is important that every facet of a multi-faceted ministry should in some way be part of or support the parish's catechetical ministry.

Pervasiveness of Catechesis

Once again, people observed that catechesis pervades every aspect of ministry. A participant found that the priests at his table perceived that "as pastors we really do very little in terms of specific focused intentional catechesis, but yet virtually everything we do serves to model and demonstrate, either poorly or well, Christianity to the community around us." Another priest referred to a discussion he and some of the other participants had had about being invited to the symposium. "But as we discussed it and talked about it more, we realized most of what we do is catechesis. But it's not the old model of the hands-on teaching CCD every week [or] working with catechists' preparation and certification, as much as it is in lots of different areas of ministry."

This concept of pervasiveness unsettled one pastor, who suggested such universality might make it difficult to focus on a particular plan or goal. He compared this broad use of catechesis to the use of the term "ministry." "Everything is called a ministry. I guess my feeling is at the moment I'm getting now as confused about what constitutes catechesis as I am at times what constitutes ministry." On the other hand, he recognized that "catechesis is at the base of almost everything we do. We begin to look at the day and any teaching, any support group—whether it be direct or indirect support to all the other ministries in the parish—appears to have some form of catechesis connected to it."

The spokesperson for another table reported that such inclusiveness requires empowerment. "If we couldn't empower and enable, we wouldn't have survived this long. . . . That was the feeling of our group. You are called upon to be present as a catechist in so many ways: to listen, to enable, to console, to support, whatever. Since all of us in the group do wear many hats we seem to be aware of the need to not only empower others, but to let them empower us because the well runs dry if we do all the empowering." Another priest added: "I think because of the broadness of the whole thing we have to reiterate the importance of allowing each member of the parish to realize their role as a catechist. For them to realize that it's not the pastor's or the pastoral staff's role to catechize, but it is actually every Christian's responsibility to catechize."

NOTES

Reflection

After analyzing your activities and reviewing these discussions, what patterns are you able to identify? What challenges are present?

A Balanced Approach

The discussion evolved into an examination of approaches to take in catechesis. It began with one priest's observation that the effective spreading of the Christian message needs to be accomplished in ways that are inviting in nature. He explained that he had experienced a heavy-handed type of approach, and to him it was a serious impediment to his Christianity. He believes this experience is not uncommon, and suggested the need to examine carefully why this happens and how to do it differently.

Reflecting on this observation, another pastor said he initially emphasizes learning by living or experiencing the faith. Reflection and articulation follow. "It's only to the degree we succeed in living and celebrating the giftedness and the faith and who we are as God's people that we have anything to reflect about anyway." His parish has tried to accentuate a model of discipleship. "And so we see what we're about in parishes is about living, about developing, about discipleship, about celebrating. And so only after that does then the educational component get plugged into the system."

Referring to the earlier reflection on catechetical approaches that may be impediments rather than implements, the pastor spoke of an imbalance. In some cases, emphasis falls predominantly on the educational component of catechesis, almost to the exclusion of a faith lived. "A twenty-four-hours-a-day, seven-days-a-week, fifty-two-weeks-a-year parish catechizing community" is effective more than one whose limited focus is only on the programmed educational model. For him, the stories of catechetical efforts that have been shared at the symposium are coming from a different paradigm, one in which education and discipleship are in a synergistic balance.

Another participant observed that although parish staffs and catechetical teams may be working out of a catechetical faith formation model, many parents of children attending catechetical programs have only experienced an educational model because that is what they encountered when they were young. The challenge, and perhaps the frustration, in this ministry comes when parents view catechesis in terms of an educational goal and not in terms of a catechetical faith formation or a transformational goal.

One of the participants described a program he has used to involve parents in the catechetical process. After prayer and some reflection at home, three families come to the rectory for dinner, which is served by parishioners who are senior citizens. After dinner the children share stories about Jesus. "It's an experience of family, it's a story of Jesus and a part of the liturgy. And you could tell afterwards that these kids had a totally different experience."

He spoke of the genuineness and excitement with which the children spoke. "They were jumping out of their seats trying to tell you the story. And the parents were sitting there like, 'I never thought this was possible.'" He concluded, saying he thinks this process could begin to involve parents in small communities. Often, parents do not participate because they are busy, but their experiences at this level might be a preparation of future small community members.

NOTES

NOTES

A fellow pastor agreed with the need for developing small groups, because he believes the church needs to gear itself much more to the adult. "If you have a young congregation in their mid 30's like mine, most of them have been out of the church for years and a very important part of helping them come back is small groups. The church doesn't resource small groups nearly well enough compared to say, the evangelical church. And there are times of the year, like Lent, when people do expect to do something special." Before Lent begins, he mails a personalized letter to each family in the parish inviting them to participate in six home sessions. This approach elicits a good response. "Last year, with 350 active families we had a couple of hundred people in the Lenten groups."

One of the last people to speak said: "I think we are overlooking what we do every Sunday. The Eucharist is the source and summit of our lives." He explained that, like others, he was not sure why he had received an invitation to the symposium, so he went back to the parish and asked the catechists, the DRE's, and the principal at the school: "What was it I did that you felt empowered you?" They told him it was the homily and the liturgy every Sunday. From the experience of the Sunday liturgy they felt renewed, reinforced, and supported.

"They said it was not uncommon that the kids who were at that liturgy, on Monday morning the first thing that they wanted to talk about was the homily. Their experience prior to that was they would be trying to present a certain image of God in the classroom," but the Sunday homily did not support their efforts. "So that when they heard from the priest, from the pulpit giving a homily that reinforced and undergirded what they were attempting to present to the class, they got life from that. It really did empower them."

He continued, explaining that "being in the Bible Belt, you learn very quickly the importance of the homily." People in that area of the country demand quality preaching, and if they do not receive it, they will turn elsewhere. In addition, he explained that seventy percent of the marriages in his state are ecumenical, inter-faith marriages and many of the non-Catholic spouses come to the liturgy on Sunday. And so often it is the homily, in addition to Eucharist, that brings people to the Church.

In conclusion, he expressed his belief that people are looking for passion. "They are looking for the word that is delivered with conviction and passion. That's power. That really is a power. I just could not let us overlook what we do every week. There's nothing that I do every week that has the potential to touch six hundred people except that one hour."

Reflection

At the end of the session, the participants were asked to list the five most important things that they do in catechetical ministry. Please take time to answer the same reflection.

The five most important things I do in catechetical ministry are:

NOTES

> *Responses from the symposium participants*
>
> **The five most important things I do in catechetical ministry as a priest.**
>
> - When interacting in a catechetical moment, maintain a positive attitude and outlook, affirming each and every attempt by others to express understanding.
>
> - Work hard to articulate the truths of our faith correctly and imaginatively.
>
> - Keep the parish focused on the primacy of the catechetical ministry.
>
> - Create a unified vision of catechetical ministry during the various programs.
>
> - Communicate daily with the DRE for planning, problem solving, and support.
>
> - Hire good, qualified people, direct them to go with their strengths, trust them, and finance their programs.
>
> - Affirm and support the volunteer catechists.
>
> - Insist on catechist formation by the DRE or by providing funds for out-of-parish programs.
>
> - Show appreciation of all those involved in various types of catechesis.
>
> - Proclaim and break open the word during the weekend and daily liturgies, which generates frequent discussion at Bible study groups and in families.
>
> - Actively call forth the gifts of the pastoral team so they function as a team.
>
> - Give quality time to myself for prayer, reading, recreation, solitude, and time away. Be sure that others take the same quality time for themselves.
>
> - Maintain an enthusiastic friendliness and an attitude of affirming acceptance at the Sunday liturgy and at all parish celebrations.

Summary

The observations about the role of the priest in catechetical ministry built naturally upon the discussions that preceded this session. In the segment on the parish, the participants spoke of parishes that display a strong sense of stewardship and entrust people with a sense of discipleship. The discussions about catechesis in the parish showed how these attributes are woven into catechesis and illustrated how all members of the church community are called to develop and strengthen their loving relationship with God throughout their lifetime and to help others do the same.

The examination of the priest in catechetical ministry further demonstrated how the parishes of the participants emphasize the community's ongoing responsibility for catechesis and its implementation, and how they incorporate stewardship and discipleship in catechetical ministry. During the discussions, some key themes emerged.

- The word. The importance of the word, of preaching well-prepared homilies as part of effective liturgical celebrations continues to surface as a critical factor in the participants' role in catechetical ministry.

- Balance. The participants' approach to catechesis has education and discipleship in a synergistic balance. Religious education comprises one component of catechesis in the parish. Although the participants participate in catechetical programs, they make sure that others are prepared and capable to handle these responsibilities.

- Limitations. The participants recognize that they alone cannot accomplish everything, and so they do not place excessive expectations on themselves. They are secure people. They are comfortable with having parishioners with complementary talents work with them, and so they actively develop lay ministry.

- Empowerment. The participants nurture the faith of parishioners and help them pass this light of faith to others. So parishioners can accomplish their catechetical mission, the priests help them recognize, develop, and use their God-given talents.

- Stewardship. In the prior sections the participants spoke of stewardship, wherein parishioners apply their time, skills, and money to serve God and neighbor. Facilitation of this stewardship, helping parishioners recognize this as part of their lived faith, comprises another aspect of the role of priests in catechetical ministry.

- Leadership. The participants help the parish develop a vision of catechesis, help the parish to focus on this vision, and then shepherd the talents of the people to help the parish carry this vision. There may be differing visions, and so the priests must minister with sensitivity.

NOTES

- Presence. The participants recognized that most of their ministry entailed catechesis. Since there are opportunities for catechesis in so much of what priests do, an important part is being present to people, talking and listening to them.

In explaining what he would say to a newly ordained priest about the role of the priest in catechesis, a participant's response offered a capsule version of the points just made. He wrote that a priest should listen, be attentive, support and encourage involvement of parishioners, nurturing them to use their gifts in service of the parish. The priest also needs to collaborate with staff members and parish leaders to enliven and strengthen the presence of the Kingdom in the parish. At the same time he should gently challenge the parish and catechists to re-think, stretch themselves, and grow to a fuller expression and understanding of their faith.

The Next Step

The next section will examine more closely the concept of the priest as empowerer of catechetical ministry.

First, review your notes and reflections as well as the material in this chapter. In order to process this information, take some time to answer the questions on the following pages. Your responses can help you examine the role of the priest in catechetical ministry in your parish. You can also use them as part of a broader planning segment in Chapter 6.

■☐ Planning Notes
■■ **The Priest in Catechetical Ministry**

In what ways does the priest affect catechesis in your parish? What are the strongest aspects of this involvement?

After reading the section on the priest in catechesis, what may be areas of potential change or addition?

What are some thoughts about strengthening existing programs?

What are some resources for change—people, material, programs?

What are some obstacles to change? How can your parish overcome them?

Chapter 4
The Priest as Empowerer of Catechetical Ministry

Introduction

Every baptized man and woman, according to his or her state in life and in the church, receives the mission to proclaim the Good News of salvation for man in Jesus Christ. Each is therefore called to exercise his or her particular responsibility. Likewise, every community is called to study deeply the concrete exigencies of the mystery of the Church and of her communion. A Message to the People of God, III

Ongoing spiritual development cannot be viewed as a part time prerogative. It is a commitment that comes with the water of baptism and the oil of confirmation, nurtured by the eucharist and the supportive community of the parish. Ongoing catechesis is essential to the life of Christians as individuals and as a Church community since all members of the Church are called to bring the Word of God to the world. The Second Vatican Council's *Decree on the Apostolate of Lay People* states: "But the laity are made to share in the priestly, prophetical and kingly office of Christ; they have therefore, in the Church and in the world, their own assignment in the mission of the whole People of God. In the concrete, their apostolate is exercised when they work at the evangelization and sanctification of men." (*Apostolicam Actuositatem*, 2)

Priests, in turn, are called both to catechize and to help people assume their role in catechetical ministry. Pope John Paul II notes this responsibility as he quotes *Lumen Gentium* in his apostolic exhortation on the laity. "Indeed, pastors know how much the lay faithful contribute to the welfare of the entire church. They also know that they themselves were not established by Christ to undertake alone the entire saving mission of the church toward the world, but they understand that is their exalted office to be shepherds of the lay faithful and also to recognize the latter's services and charisms that all according to their proper roles may cooperate in this common undertaking with one heart. (*Lumen Gentium,* 30)" (*Christifideles Laici*, 32)

Priests must identify and nurture those who have the charism of being catechists, putting special interest in caring for their initial and permanent formation. "To the extent possible, the priest must be the *catechist of catechists*, forming in these a veritable community of disciples of the Lord which serves as a point of reference for those receiving instruction." (*Directory for the Life and Ministry of Priests*, 47) The *National Catechetical Directory* explains: "The person of the catechist is the medium in which the message of the faith is incarnated." (*NCD*, Conclusion)

Catechists, therefore, possess a role of great importance. Are they able to fulfill this role with conviction? Can they convey the wisdom and confidence of faith that inspires others and touches their hearts? Can they follow the example of Jesus? "When Jesus finished these words, the crowds were astonished at his teaching, for he taught them as one having authority, and not as their scribes." (Matthew 7:28–29) How can priests help people take hold of this responsibility to catechize with the power of their faith? In other words, how can priests empower those in catechetical ministry?

NOTES

NOTES

People sometimes misunderstand the concept of empowerment when used in the context of the Church and catechesis. Some feel threatened by the thought of lay empowerment, believing the clergy will forfeit authority. Others desire it, because they mistakenly perceive empowerment as a source of influence. Both perceptions are misplaced, grounded in a temporal perspective, not a spiritual one. "When man accepts the Spirit of Christ, God introduces him to a way of life completely new. It empowers a man to share in God's own life. He is joined to the Father and to Christ in a vital union which not even death can break." (*Basic Teachings for Catholic Religious Education*, 14)

The Spirit is the true empowerer. "Catechesis, which is growth in faith and the maturing of Christian life towards its fullness, is consequently a work of the Holy Spirit, a work that he alone can initiate and sustain in the Church." (*Catechesi Tradendae*, 72) Mary and the disciples were empowered by the Spirit on Pentecost, and so all members of the Church must be open to the same Spirit and to the same results. As the American bishops wrote in their plan and strategy for evangelization in the United States, *Go and Make Disciples*: "Jesus was led by the Spirit of God to a life of preaching and service, to the giving of himself in sacrifice. Jesus Christ sends that same Spirit upon everyone who is baptized in his name. For we have all gone down into the water of Christ and have all been anointed to bring Good News and be true disciples. [cf. Romans 6:3-4] We have all received his Spirit. This is not a Spirit of timidity or fear, but a bold Spirit of life, truth, joy, and grace." (*Go and Make Disciples*, page 10)

Priests help people grow in faith through catechesis in all its forms. They also help people realize that they must not conceal the light of faith under a bushel basket. "Just so, your light must shine before others, that they may see your good deeds and glorify your heavenly Father." (Matthew 5:16) They must help catechists gain confidence in themselves so that, as in the parable recorded by Matthew, they use and develop their talents wisely and not be timid and bury them. (cf. Matthew 25: 14–30)

At the same time, priests must themselves be open to the Spirit and have the confidence and security to allow the Spirit to work in others. "The Church, therefore, does not accomplish this discernment only through the pastors, who teach in the name and with the power of Christ, but also through the laity: Christ 'made them his witnesses and gave them understanding of the faith and the grace of speech (cf. Acts 2:17–18; Revelation. 19:10), so that the power of the Gospel might shine forth in their daily social and family life.' (*Lumen Gentium*, 35)" (*Familiaris Consortio*, 5)

The empowerment of catechetical ministry is an example of responding to the movement of the Spirit in the life of the Church.

Synopsis

The examination of empowerment began on the first day of the symposium and continued until it adjourned. In the first three segments of the symposium, the participants examined parishes and the role of catechesis in the parishes, and then discussed the role that priests play in catechesis. In the fourth segment, the participants continued this analysis of the empowerment of catechetical ministry, building on the information developed during the previous three sessions.

The participants observed three roleplays representing encounters a pastor may typically have in the context of catechetical ministry. In roleplay, two people assume the role of a character in a loosely defined situation. Observation of this interaction can provide insights on several levels. In this case it was used to facilitate discussion concerning the situation and the actions taken, the pastor's relation with catechists, and the dynamics of empowerment. You will have the opportunity to participate in the same roleplays. If this is not possible, you can reflect on your own experience and compare it with the experiences of the symposium's participants.

The participants also examined their spiritual journeys and the people and experiences that helped lead them to the priesthood. This exploration helped them identify common elements in their ministerial growth. You will also have the opportunity to consider your ministerial journey.

Reflection Questions

Before reviewing the roleplays and the observations they generated, please take time to complete the last group of reflection questions on the following pages, drawing upon your wisdom and parish experience.

After answering the questions, continue with the rest of the chapter. As before, continue to use the responses from the symposium as benchmarks for comparison with your responses. Enter into the proceedings and consider how you would have responded to the comments offered. Use the margins for notes.

■■ Reflection Questions
■■ The Priest as Empowerer of Catechetical Ministry

In catechetical ministry, describe how you personally influence:

- Parents

- Families

- Single People

- The Parish Staff

- The DRE

- Catechists

- Teachers

■■ Reflection Questions
■■ **The Priest as Empowerer of Catechetical Ministry** (Continued)

How much time do you personally devote to:

- Catechesis/Religious Education

- Meeting with the DRE

- Catechists

- Catechist Formation

■■ Reflection Questions
■■ **The Priest as Empowerer of Catechetical Ministry** (Continued)

Create/describe your parish's "catechetical portrait." Who/what is/are in the picture you would paint? Be as open-ended or as specific as you wish.

■■ Reflection Questions
■■ **The Priest as Empowerer of Catechetical Ministry** (Continued)

Now focus on how you empower <u>one</u> catechist from your parish. For this person, ask yourself:

- How do I support her or him?

- How do I provide catechetical opportunities?

- How do I acknowledge her or his gifts to the parish?

- What kind of staff support does our parish provide?

- When do I pray with this catechist?

■■ Reflection Questions
■■ **The Priest as Empowerer of Catechetical Ministry** (Continued)

- How does my relationship with this and other catechists influence my preaching?

- What have I learned from this catechist?

- What might I do differently as a result of ministering with this catechist?

- What might I do the same as a result of ministering with this catechist?

Responses from the symposium participants

Focusing on how you empower <u>one</u> catechist from your parish:

How do you support the catechist?

- I meet with her at least once a month as a mentor, encourage her to explore new ways of doing her ministry, and help her process and evaluate her ministry. I connect her with the parish DRE and publicize her position and ministry responsibilities.

- I have encouraged her spiritual growth and have been a companion to her on her faith journey. I have been available to discuss her efforts in ministry and to lend support and counsel, and I have encouraged her to continue her formation as a catechist.

- I work through the DRE and I listen and encourage the catechist in her ministry. The catechist also comes to me for spiritual direction.

- I greet him warmly at each meeting, compliment him on his work, and let him know how much I appreciate his competence and how much I count on him. I encourage him to take extra time for his family when there have been a lot of demands on his time during the evenings. I give time and resources so he can further himself in his area.

- I let her know that her ministry is important and valuable. I also take time to listen to her critiques of the program and to let her know that I consider her very accomplished in her work.

- My support comes by being there, by affirming her, by thanking her for a well done job, and by getting her the things she needs to teach.

- I support her by providing her with on-going catechetical opportunities, communicating with her, praying with her and her family, and affirming her strengths and challenging her weaknesses.

How do you provide catechetical opportunities?

- The parish sends her each year to the annual three day Religious Education Congress. I also sponsor her for other catechetical seminars and workshops when offered and when relevant to her ministry.

- I hire a strong DRE. I personally and financially encourage continued catechetical training and spiritual formation.

- Catechetical opportunities are always there. I try to help others to recognize the opportunities and believe they can make a difference.

- We publicize the opportunities for Conferences and local Diocesan events and we pay for their attendance. I personally do not do the groundwork for this, I simply encourage it.

- I look at short term tasks or programs and personally invite her to participate and/or facilitate. I invite her to come to me with her ideas, her hopes and wishes gleaned from her relationship with parishioners.

NOTES

How Priests Empower

During one of the exercises in the previous segment of the symposium the participants were asked: "What is it that you can legitimately say you do to empower catechists or catechetical leaders in the parish?" Since the insights that were expressed helped lay the foundation for the roleplays in this segment and are so closely tied to the topic, the responses are covered here. They are not recorded in order of importance or priority.

Catechetical Development

One pastor said he encourages people to attend diocesan formation programs, such as the three year Master Catechist program, diocesan workshops and Congresses. Another invites the diocese to use parish facilities to conduct programs. Parishioners can easily attend, and they don't have to pay a fee. If programs are in other locations, the DRE organizes transportation using the parish vans. He also shared his personal experience in parishes where schools closed: "Those people who were catechists were now front and center as leaders."

Trust

A priest explained that he empowers catechists through support and trust. He likes to use ideas that catechists offer. He explained, "Trust yourself, trust the Lord as a part of that, and go with it. It will succeed, and if it doesn't, that's where evaluation comes in. But don't question it and talk yourself out of it. Just take the risk, be the dreamer and go with it." As the *Decree on the Apostolate of Lay People* points out: "It is for the pastors to pass judgment on the authenticity and good use of these gifts, not certainly with a view to quenching the Spirit but to testing everything and keeping what is good (cf. 1 Thessalonians 5:12, 19, 21)." (*Apostolicam Actuositatem,* 3)

However, another pastor added that trusting people requires a positive set of assumptions about human nature. "That it's resilient, creative, capable of responsibilities. Some people, however, harbor negative sets of assumptions. I believe so many people are distrusting of widespread ministry because they essentially are distrusting of people in general."

Affirmation

One pastor asked people why they thought he empowered catechists. "They said that mainly because I, in working with them over the years, affirmed them. I knew them by name and I called people by name and named what they were doing as ministry. And they found that empowering."

Financial Support

Speaking of financial support, a pastor said he attempts to insure that funds are allocated for anything reasonable in the area of catechesis. He also explained that he visits classes and is present for the catechists. Another pastor stated that he empowers catechists by selecting the right personnel for the full time staff.

Personal Development

One priest, referring to catechetical ministry in a parish with many recent immigrants, cited a need "to meet people where they are." In order for people to become skilled leaders, it is necessary to help them overcome challenges they may have in certain areas. "So we start from there, we start from allowing them to learn certain learning skills, reading, writing and expressing themselves, standing up in public in their own language before we even worry about whether they know English or not. So that once they feel confident in their own unique expression, in the cultural expression, hopefully they'll be able to start telling their stories, something more intimate. So I think with faith development comes also the very basic human development aspect."

Respect Time

A participant said one important aspect of empowering catechists is to respect their limited time. Therefore, the parish schedules catechetical sessions to fit into the rhythm of the lives of the parishioners—either before or after Mass on Sunday. The pastor believes that this attention to time is a key to the success of the catechetical program, which has virtually no catechist turnover.

Perception

In one parish the pastor calls the catechetical program the School of Religion in order to put it on an equal basis with the parish grade school and high school in the eyes of the parishioners.

Enjoyment

One pastor believes it is necessary to maintain a component of enjoyment for the catechists and for those they catechize. He said the catechists in his parish like to play together, so, as he expressed it, "there is a heavy social content." Amusement park trips and social gatherings complement the catechetical program. "I believe to be people of joy, to enjoy is a necessary and fundamental component of our Christianity."

NOTES

Responses from the symposium participants

How do your actions empower catechists?

- We empower catechists directly through our involvement in the formation programs for catechists and in the enrichment programs for them. Indirectly, we empower the catechists by being part of the Religious Education Board, by forming a sense of ministry within the parish and urging people to find their proper role in the parish, by encouraging teachers in what they are doing as being an important task in the parish, and by visits to the classrooms and presence at catechetical functions.

- The environment present in the parish shows that the catechetical ministry is an important priority of the parish. The presence of the pastor at many of the catechetical meetings and actual classes shows the importance of the catechetical role.

- The DRE is encouraged to see that catechists are trained and certified. I know and call the catechists by name and I go on retreats with them. Catechists are recognized and empowered as ministers on Catechetical Sunday.

- My actions demonstrate that all baptized Christians are interconnected and responsible for sharing the Good News. By preaching, teaching and encouraging catechists to participate in updating, I demonstrate the importance of the ministry of catechist, the importance and need for their ministry, and the interdependence of our ministries.

- The importance of the role of catechists in the big picture is clear. They are part of a team/partnership effort. It keeps their task within focus. I publicly acknowledge their contribution, its importance, and the need for total parish recognition. I compliment them for a life well shared.

- There are several ways: by letting them know of the high value I place on their ministry, by providing staff and resources needed to enable them, by recognizing them before the parish for their valuable contribution, and by being available to assist them personally in the classroom.

- I give my catechists the freedom to be themselves. Their textbooks convey information. The teachers chosen are people of strong and balanced faith. They convey their faith and maturity to the children.

- My actions empower catechists by allowing them to take ownership of their ministry and the responsibility that comes with it.

- We need stronger and more models of lay ministry. Thus, I try to help my catechists see their efforts as a mission rather than as a task, that is, we are responding to God's presence in our lives. My efforts revolve around four key issues: recognition, growth opportunities, stabilization, and professionalism.

NOTES

Reflection

How are catechists empowered in your parish? What impact does this have on the catechetical ministry? In what ways could catechists be empowered more effectively?

NOTES

Three Roleplay Scenarios

Three roleplays were used to help the participants examine the empowering role priests play in catechetical ministry. In roleplay, people assume roles in loosely defined situations, providing an opportunity to observe lifelike circumstances in order to gain insight into attitudes and behaviors. For the symposium roleplays, three pairs of volunteers played the roles in front of the group. After observing each roleplay, the participants shared their insights and opinions.

In each of the roleplays, a pastor is speaking with a person about catechetical ministry. The roles and the issues are:

- Roleplay 1: Roles: Associate Pastor and Pastor
  Issue: Responsibility for catechetical program

- Roleplay 2: Roles: DRE and Pastor
  Issue: Parental involvement in sacramental programs

- Roleplay 3: Roles: Parishioner and Pastor
  Issue: Potential catechist

The purpose of the roleplays is not to evaluate interview skills or the ease at which tasks are accomplished. The roleplays should help you focus on the catechetical program, the relation between the pastor and others in catechetical ministry, and the presence of empowerment.

Though they may include the same characters and address the same issues, no two roleplays will be the same. The outcomes depend on the players, how they see the roles, and how they react to each other. In every case, however, insights can be drawn. Every roleplay has two groups of participants: the people who are the players and the people who observe. Each person brings a different perspective to the analysis and discussion.

Therefore, try to participate in the roleplays yourself before reading the summaries of the symposium's roleplays and the observations that followed. If you are using this book in conjunction with a staff or other group, finding a roleplay partner will be fairly easy. If you are completing this workbook independently, think of some people who could participate with you. This may include someone on staff, a catechist, or a friend.

If you choose not to roleplay, or if there is no opportunity to do so at this time, approach the material as if you were going to participate in the roleplay as an observer. This will help you consider ways in which you would approach the situation, and it will also give you insight as to how the roles were played during the symposium. Only read the symposium roleplay synopsis and the symposium roleplay observations after you have participated in that roleplay as a player, observer, or reader.

Components

Each roleplay section contains these components:

- Role Descriptions. If you are playing one of the roles, only read the part you will play. If you are an observer or reader, please read both roles.

  The descriptions in the roleplays are fairly general so the information can be adapted to a variety of situations. Therefore, before the roleplay begins, the roleplayers or a third person may want to provide additional information that might enhance the roleplay (for example, how many families there are in the parish).

- Opportunity for Roleplay.

- Opportunity for Discussion.

- Roleplay Reflection Questions. Whether you are actively participating in the roleplay as a player or observer, or you are reading the roles on your own, these questions can help you reflect on the roleplay or the issue at hand. You can compare this with what might happen in your own parish.

- Synopsis of Symposium Roleplay. This is a summary of each roleplay as it occurred during the symposium. The roleplay synopsis is not meant to be a model, but rather a record of the unrehearsed roleplay that occurred during the symposium. Since the symposium discussions are based upon this activity, it will give you a point of reference, and it will also provide additional opportunity for reflection and comparison.

- Symposium Roleplay Observations. This section summarizes the thoughts of the participants about the roleplay that they observed.

- Reflection Questions.

Roleplay Guidelines

There are two categories of people involved in roleplay—the people who play the roles and observers who watch them. These guidelines provide a general direction for each group. If your are not participating in a roleplay, please read these guidelines as if your were an observer.

Observers or Readers

If you are part of a group and will be observing the roleplay, or if you are not going to be part of any roleplay at this time, please read the instructions for both roles. As you observe the roleplay, use the space for notes to record thoughts or questions that may arise during the roleplay, or if you are not participating, as you read and consider the roles.

Please also read the roleplay guidelines for the roleplayers.

NOTES

Roleplayers

Each roleplay has two roles, and the instructions for each appear at the beginning of each roleplay section.

- If you are going to be one of the roleplay participants, only read the role that you will play.
- Take some time to think about the situation and the role. There may be parallels in your own experience, or you may have heard of similar situations. Draw upon this experience.
- The roleplay should last no less than ten minutes.

There are some guidelines that are helpful in any roleplay.

- Stay in the role throughout the entire period. If you think of something you want to discuss, write a note to yourself. It can be part of the debriefing that follows.
- Be serious about the roleplay. Jokes will distract from the purpose at hand.
- In order for the roleplay to be effective, be realistic. You should only portray something that would naturally happen. Avoid raising obstacles or proposing solutions that would not ordinarily occur.

Once the roleplay has ended, the players and observers should talk about what happened during the roleplay. The purpose is not to evaluate interview skills or the ease at which tasks are accomplished. If you are one of the players, do not worry about making "mistakes." The discussion should focus on the parish catechetical program, the relation between the pastor and others in catechetical ministry, and the presence of empowerment. You can use the questions that follow each scenario for further discussion and reflection.

Roleplay Procedure, Recap

- Prepare
- Roleplay
- Discuss
- Reflect
- Review
- Reflect

Roleplay 1 – Responsibility for the Catechetical Program

Role: Associate Pastor

In this roleplay, the pastor is meeting with the newly ordained associate pastor to discuss responsibility for the parish's catechetical programs.

You are an associate pastor who has just been assigned to the parish. The pastor has asked to meet with you about assuming responsibility for catechesis in the parish. In the past, the parish had a full-time professional DRE. Currently, the catechetical programs are administered by a volunteer skilled in administration but not in theology or catechetical theory.

You are newly ordained and are eager to minister in the parish, but are unsure of what will be expected of you. You do not know if you will have as much time to devote to catechesis as you would prefer, so you are a bit concerned about "high expectations."

Preparation Notes

Have you experienced a situation like this or have you heard of something similar? What did you do? What would you have done?

NOTES

Roleplay 1 – Responsibility for the Catechetical Program

Role: Pastor

In this roleplay, the pastor is meeting with the newly ordained associate pastor to discuss responsibility for the parish's catechetical programs.

You are the pastor of the parish. You have asked to meet with the newly ordained associate pastor about assuming responsibility for catechesis in the parish. In the past, the parish had a full-time professional DRE. Currently, the catechetical programs are administered by a volunteer skilled in administration but not in theology or catechetical theory.

As pastor, how will you proceed? What will you say to the associate about the parish? About catechesis in the parish? About being part of the parish's catechetical team? You hope that the associate pastor will be very enthusiastic about accepting responsibility for the catechetical needs of the parish.

Preparation Notes

Have you experienced a situation like this or have you heard of something similar? What did you do? What would you have done?

Post-roleplay Reflection

These questions can help you reflect on your own roleplay and observations.

In the roleplay, what responsibility for catechesis was given to the associate pastor? What authority to carry out this responsibility did the associate pastor receive?

How might this situation be handled in your parish?

NOTES

Roleplay 1: Responsibility for the Catechetical Program

Symposium Synopsis

After initial pleasantries, the pastor asked the associate pastor to become director of the parish's catechetical program. The associate reacted hesitantly and asked for clarification. For example, he asked about the amount of time required and about personnel and financial resources. The pastor replied that his role would be Director of Religious Education for preschool through the confirmation programs, and that "it is a program totally given over to you. You are in charge." He also explained that there is a budget that can be modified, and that there will be secretarial and office support.

The associate expressed concern that the volunteer who ran the program had no formal training in catechesis or theology, wondering if the program needed to be rebuilt. The pastor explained that the volunteer is a teacher, and drew upon those skills. He said the program has a structure for eight hundred students in kindergarten through sixth grade, two hundred students in seventh and eighth grades, and two hundred in the confirmation program. The pastor sees the real weakness as catechist formation, and he does not think the coordination of the program is not as effective as it should be.

The pastor said he would like smaller classes with two catechists in every class. He told the associate pastor that he would have the facilities and funds he needed. When asked what he meant, the pastor replied that the budget for catechesis would be based on the assessment of the entire staff, and emphasized that the entire staff wants a good catechetical program. The associate pastor felt that the job description indicated the need for a full time person, and he asked to be assigned exclusively to catechetics. The pastor declined, but assured him that directing the catechetical program would be an important responsibility of the associate pastor. "And if within a year or two years it became very obvious that the task was a larger one, then we would look into the budget to see what could be done."

The associate replied that six months might be a more reasonable period for assessment. The pastor said that this program was part of a larger catechesis and ministry in the parish, and that the entire staff is part of the overall evaluation and budgeting process. If it becomes clear that changes have to be made before two years, then "we'll do whatever we can to make it work."

At this point the roleplay ended.

Observations

The comments about the first roleplay fell into the following categories:
- Extent of Authority
- The Role of the DRE
- Background and Training

The Role of the DRE

After the roleplay, one person observed that much of the discussion centered on catechetical programs for children, and that there was little if any mention of adult catechesis or other types of catechetical programs. The priest playing the role of the pastor explained that he was drawing upon his own experience for the role. In his parish the DRE is responsible for children's catechesis while another person handles adult catechesis. He attempted to make this distinction in the roleplay by explaining to the associate pastor that he would be responsible for preschool through confirmation.

One participant observed that twenty-five years ago he was a newly ordained priest in a similar situation. However, at the present time all the parishes in his diocese that have an associate also have DRE's. Therefore, a pastor would never ask the associate to be responsible for the catechetical programs. A professional person would be hired to do that.

Responding to this, another pastor said that many parishes may not be able to afford to hire a DRE, and so they have a part time volunteer who needs direction. In any case, he believes it is important for priests to serve in catechetical programs. He finds that new priests sometimes lack the skills to direct a catechetical program. This pastor also believes that some priests do not want to be part of the parish's catechetical program. "They say, well we now hire people to do that. We don't have to worry about that." He would not appoint an associate pastor as director, but he would want him to have some knowledge about the program and would have him participate in it.

Another participant reflected that he sees something wrong with a parish that has one thousand children in the catechetical program and did not have a DRE. However, he agreed with the earlier comment that it is very important to have the associate intimately involved in the catechetical program.

Extent of Authority

The discussion also focused on the components of responsibility and authority. One priest observed that in his experience as an associate, he was given responsibility without any authority. Practically everything had to be approved by the pastor. He appreciated the fact that the associate pastor in the roleplay had responsibility for the entire program, but he thought it would be difficult to commit to a program for two years when that may not be the area of his strongest skills. Another priest observed that it is "great to know what you can do, but what are the things that you can't do?" He felt the pastor here did not set any limitations, and it is important to give some boundaries.

Another priest recalled being in a situation similar to that in the roleplay. He was the pastor. An associate, who had been ordained for approximately twelve years and who had previously been a teacher, was assigned to the parish. There was no director, so the associate took over the catechetical program. Money was limited, but the participant wanted the associate to have the freedom to devote time to catechesis so he offered to assume any duties the associate had to give up in order to favor the catechetical program. The participant felt that this arrangement worked well.

NOTES

Background and Training

Since the role of the priest in the community is irreplaceable, it is essential that candidates for the priesthood have a solid formation in catechesis. This is particularly true with respect to adult catechesis, for which they need to learn to direct and collaborate with lay catechesis.

Adult Catechesis in the Christian Community, 83

A newly appointed pastor explained he offered his comments from the perspective of a person fresh from the position of associate pastor. As a newly ordained priest, he found it difficult to be given tasks without first getting to know the parish and getting to know what his abilities were in terms of the needs of the parish. He would have liked to have been in the position a few months before sitting down with the pastor to talk about the needs of the parish and how he could address them with the skills he possessed.

One pastor, recalling his seminary experience twenty-five years before, remembered that training in catechetics was fairly minimal. He would have found it overwhelming to come into a parish community and learn that he was responsible for the entire catechetical program since he had not received training to deal with issues of catechetics in the parish. He wondered whether this topic is covered more thoroughly in the seminaries today.

Reflection

What role does the priest in your parish play in catechesis?

Roleplay 2 – Parental Involvement in Sacramental Programs

Role: DRE

The scenario of the second roleplay has the pastor and the DRE meeting to discuss the lack of family participation in sacramental preparation. Many attempts have been made to increase parental involvement, but there has been little change.

You are the DRE and are meeting with the pastor to discuss the parish's lack of family involvement in sacramental preparation. It seems that despite all the efforts of the parish, the same "faithful few" parents attend the preparation meetings. Although you and the pastor have discussed providing home-based opportunities for sacramental catechesis, neither of you was convinced such an approach would be worth the risk.

However, you wonder why families have not participated in your parish's creative sacramental programs, and you are searching for alternative ways to get people enthusiastically involved. You have been in the position two years and are well-received by parishioners at parish gatherings, but you cannot seem to get things moving with family involvement for sacramental preparation. You are frustrated and unable to predict the outcomes of your efforts. At this point you want to try an at-home approach to engage families in sacramental preparation.

Preparation Notes

Have you experienced a situation like this or have you heard of something similar? What did you do? What would you have done?

Roleplay 2 – Parental Involvement in Sacramental Programs

Role: Pastor

The scenario of the second roleplay has the pastor and the DRE meeting to discuss the lack of family participation in sacramental preparation. Many attempts have been made to increase parental involvement, but there has been little change.

The DRE is meeting with you to discuss the parish's lack of family involvement in the parish's sacramental preparation. It seems that despite all the efforts of the parish, the same "faithful few" parents attend their preparation meetings. In the past you and the DRE have discussed providing home-based opportunities for sacramental catechesis in the parish, but neither of you was convinced that such an approach would be worth the risk.

When you hired the DRE, you indicated that one of the objectives was to ensure that parents attend the parish's catechetical programs. Now you might be asked to consider an at-home approach. You are worried that the program might not work. At the same time you are very concerned about the DRE, the catechists, and the families. You know the DRE is completely devoted to catechetical ministry, and do not understand why families are not involved in sacramental preparation.

Preparation Notes

Have you experienced a situation like this or have you heard of something similar? What did you do? What would you have done?

NOTES

Post-roleplay Reflection

These questions can help you reflect on your own roleplay and observations.

What do you see as the central challenge of this situation? Are there similar challenges in your parish?

What solutions did the pastor and the DRE develop in this roleplay? What others would you have suggested?

NOTES

Roleplay 2: Parental Involvement in Sacramental Programs

Symposium Synopsis

The meeting began as the DRE explained that she and the catechists have worked to prepare parents to be part of the children's sacramental formation, but that only a few parents participate. She wanted to discuss some creative approaches to this lack of participation.

The pastor inquired if the DRE had uncovered any reasons for the lack of participation through conversations with parents and catechists. She replied that for First Communion preparation, catechists called parents and sent notes home, and some catechists visited parents in an attempt to carry out this preparation in the home. The DRE said the catechists want to continue home visits for sacramental preparation, so she asked if these could replace the meetings at the church.

The pastor expressed concern, saying the group process of meetings provides helpful input and sharing. He said a lack of solutions for poor attendance does not mean that preparation will work if "we just send it home." Expressing similar frustration, the DRE explained that parents frequently tell her that they meant to go to the meetings, but something came up or they forgot. She finds that parents often ask for follow-up. Although she hears the same reasons, the DRE believes the parents are interested. She thinks some underestimate their ability to catechize their children, so perhaps home visits would be the best way to help them.

The pastor wondered if so many parents find reasons not to participate in group sessions designed to help them catechize their children, can they be expected to be prepared to catechize at home? Although hesitant, the DRE feels the risk is worthwhile. She presented a plan to divide the parish into blocks and to have three teams of two catechists to work with the parents in these divisions. The pastor suggested that she organize a meeting with the catechists and families in one of the blocks to solicit their reactions to this proposal. He then asked about implementation. She answered that after examination and design, they could start the first reconciliation program in September.

The pastor asked if, after examination, they decided against this new approach, would there be time to review the current method and develop other creative ideas. The DRE suggested they poll some parents who recently experienced sacramental preparation to identify obstacles that may exist. Perhaps the parents could also give some insight as to what would work well with other parents in their neighborhoods. The pastor backed the DRE's at-home proposal, but said she must be sure that she, the parents, and the catechists have a firm sense of direction. The DRE was happy to be able to work with the catechists on this approach.

With this, the roleplay ended.

Observations

The Church community also keeps its promise to parents by providing programs intended specifically to help them in their catechetical role. Such programs focus on the task of parents in relation to particular moments or issues in the child's religious life, such as sacramental preparation and moral development. They also seek to familiarize parents with the stages in children's growth and the relevance these have for catechesis.

National Catechetical Directory, 212

The participants' observations and comments fall into three categories:

- Parental Motivation
- Mandatory Participation
- Unified Purpose

Parental Motivation

The first observation came from a pastor who explained that he did not observe any motivation on the part of the parents. He feels people sometimes have an attitude that whether or not they attend any meetings, their child will make First Communion. So they think, "What difference does it make whether or not I'm there?" Though the pastor and the DRE may talk about creative approaches, the participant thinks optional meetings are at the heart of the matter. His parish offers options, eight or nine courses, for the parents. However, participation is mandatory. He felt the situation in the parish, as played in the roleplay, did not have enough structure, and so more creative ideas may not have solved the problem.

The next pastor to speak agreed with the need for mandatory participation, but he also saw the need to seek different approaches when people do not respond. Rather than just continuing with the status quo and wondering why people do not participate, he said change can make a difference. The participant explained that, although this idea seems pretty simple, he often sees parishes get bogged down in their program without exploring alternatives.

Another participant observed that in parishes that have made the transition to home preparation, there seems to be an initial and even enduring resistance on the part of school parents. Because they pay tuition and send their children to a Catholic school, some people expect the school to provide preparation for sacraments. He has found that it takes a lot of catechesis—personal conversation with parents, letters, etc.—to help parents understand that the family is the primary religious educator. He explained that it takes a great deal of work with the parents.

He continued to say that this preparation is mandatory in his parish. He observed that it is easier to mandate this for First Eucharist because people want to be sure that their children celebrate their First Eucharist. However, he does not think people feel the same responsibility or obligation for the other sacraments.

NOTES

Mandatory Participation

The ongoing discussion of the benefits of mandatory parental participation sparked a lively discussion. One participant commented: "We seem to be a contradictory people." He referred to a prior discussion about a balanced approach to catechesis. He questioned the wisdom of making the participation of parents a prerequisite of the child's reception of a sacrament. He thinks this would convey contradictory messages. On one hand parents are told they are the primary catechists of their children, yet on the other hand they encounter mandatory classes that imply a suspicion that they are not doing the job. He thinks some of this stance needs to be rethought.

This position was questioned by another pastor who asked: "Did Jesus make no demands on people?" The first pastor explained that he did not mean to exclude demands, but to consider different ways of making demands. When a couple presents their child for a sacrament, instead of requiring their attendance at a program, perhaps consider the possibility that the parents might do a better job themselves at home. Consider the options that are open to them.

The second pastor responded: "But ours is a covenant faith and if they come to the community, the community has some responsibility towards them." The first pastor explained that he was only cautioning against setting up rigid requirements. He feels that instead of helping people come to the Lord, mandatory meetings may actually pose obstacles.

A third priest observed that, in his experience, the vast majority of committed Catholic people do not object to programs that require their participation. He thinks the real challenge comes when any demands are placed on people who are not committed, asking their participation in formation to acquaint them, to affect them, and to ask a commitment from them. However, when appropriate he will ask for some commitment. For example, if parents want their child to receive First Communion, they must attend the requisite classes.

He continued to say if uncommitted people are in the group preparing for Confirmation, he believes they should show some element of personal commitment. If they want to get married later on, he tells them "if you're old enough to get married, you're old enough to make some type of decision about a relationship to the Church."

Unified Purpose

One priest thought the pastor put the DRE on the defensive by constantly asking questions. He observed that the pastor never asked how he could be of service, what could he do, or how he could help. The participant explained that this bothered him because it is not the problem of the DRE. It is a joint problem. It is the parish's problem. He did not think the conversation went in that direction.

Reflection

What is the degree of parental involvement in sacramental preparation in your parish? What is the approach to parents' participation?

NOTES

> **Working with people in catechetical ministry – some reflections**
>
> *Responses from the symposium participants*
>
> **Focusing on how you empower <u>one</u> catechist from your parish:**
>
> **What have you learned from this catechist?**
>
> - I have seen how this person's ministry touches the rest of her family. She has drawn the best out of them. In sharing her faith with others, she shares herself in so many other ways. She has a healthy vision of the Church and Church ministry because of her ministry as a catechist.
>
> - He has taught me not to overreact to negative situations. He has shown me how to cherish each moment as a graced moment from God.
>
> - The Spirit is always and forever present in each of us in a unique and challenging way.
>
> - Her continuous commitment to that ministry is very supportive to my understanding of commitment to priesthood. There is a generosity of spirit in her ministry which I admire and find exemplary for myself.
>
> - She has often been a sounding board for my critiques or my complaints and I find her insights to be most valuable and to be a corrective to my own viewpoint.
>
> - Young people even at the doctoral level have quite a different approach to Roman Catholic Christianity and catechetics than I did.
>
> - Patience; faith is a joyful gift and people can find self-worth by using their gifts.
>
> - Some of the difficulties of teaching and living as a wife and mother. Her love and generosity humble me.
>
> - Never to think too highly of myself and my own "expertise" because daily life and the lived experience of people is a powerful, grace-filled educational tool. Trust that God is working in and through all kinds of people.
>
> - How to be gracious and go the extra step.
>
> - Commitment to ministry and personal growth in faith; recognition of gifts and generosity in sharing them.
>
> - I have grown in faith and hope through the inspiration of her faith.
>
> - The ministry of the laity is concretized for me. The relationship lets me know where my people are in relation to understanding the word. There are many gifts but the same Spirit.

Roleplay 3 – Potential Catechist

Role: Parishioner

In the third roleplay, the pastor is approached by a parishioner who wants to volunteer as a catechist in a program that currently has eight catechist vacancies.

It is recruitment weekend for the catechetical program. During the homily the pastor said there are eight groups without a leader! The pastor is now greeting parishioners after the celebration of the Eucharist. Finally, you decide to talk with him about volunteering.

You have been thinking about volunteering to be a catechist, but never got around to it. You wonder if you are qualified and hesitate at first to approach your pastor. But then you think of the parish's needs, and knowing all you were taught as a child, decide to offer your services.

Preparation Notes

Have you experienced a situation like this or have you heard of something similar? What did you do? What would you have done?

NOTES

Roleplay 3 – Potential Catechist

Role: Pastor

In the third roleplay, the pastor is approached by a parishioner who wants to volunteer as a catechist in a program that currently has eight catechist vacancies.

It's finally here! Recruitment weekend for the catechetical program. As you greet parishioners after the celebration of the Eucharist, you are thinking of ways to recruit more catechists – there are eight groups without a leader! Finally, a parishioner approaches you to talk about volunteering.

You know you need seven more catechists if the person who is approaching you volunteers. You are eager to have the volunteer serve, but are unsure of the person's training, background, or regular availability.

Preparation Notes

Have you experienced a situation like this or have you heard of something similar? What did you do? What would you have done?

Post-roleplay Reflection

These questions can help you reflect on your own roleplay prior to continuing with the material.

Think about what happened in the roleplay. How would you have handled the situation differently?

How would a similar situation be handled in your parish?

Roleplay 3: Potential Catechist

Symposium Synopsis

The parishioner approached the pastor to volunteer as a catechist, explaining that he wanted to do so before but was unsure about his qualifications. He believes he is qualified because of the religious training he received as a child. He referred to the ten commandments, the precepts of the church, and the Baltimore Catechism. Although he has had no religious education since childhood, he thinks he has much to offer the children.

After listening intently to the parishioner's background, the pastor asked if the primary reason for volunteering was the desire to help the children. The parishioner replied that the youth of today are confused "because things are too loose. I think we should come down on the ten commandments and really help them understand what God wants of them." The pastor then reflected on the comments about education, the Baltimore Catechism, and the precepts of the church. He told the parishioner he appreciated his enthusiasm, and asked him to talk a little bit about his faith experience.

The parishioner explained that after the service he married and began a family. He and his wife sent their children to Catholic school. He said this pleased him because the school took care of their children's Catholic education. He and his wife were not too involved, and in fact their familiarity with the Second Vatican Council was limited to the changes in the liturgy. Now, with the children grown and out of the house, he has extra time and would like to help the church as a catechist.

Once again, the pastor told the parishioner that he appreciated his enthusiasm for becoming a catechist. However, the priest explained that he did not think it would be best for the parishioner or the parish if he immediately appointed the parishioner as a catechist. He told the parishioner he would like to spend some time talking with him to learn more about his interests and determine how he can best utilize his gifts and skills. The pastor also explained that it is important to share a vision of catechesis and religious education.

The parishioner was somewhat puzzled and annoyed. He said he did not understand why the pastor was not more enthusiastic, especially with eight catechist vacancies. "I'm a lifetime Catholic and I have a good foundation and I don't quite understand what's going on." The pastor replied that he really appreciated the parishioner's desire to be a catechist. However, the vision of the Church today, rooted in the Second Vatican Council, may be different from the parishioner's expectations and approach. He asked the parishioner if he would be open to do some reflection and reading, after which they would talk again about volunteering as a catechist.

At this point, the roleplay ended.

Observations

Yet effective catechesis also depends a great deal on human effort: on planning, performance, and evaluation, on personal qualities and commitment. Especially does it depend upon the faith, hope, and love of catechists, responding to God's grace by growing in these virtues and ministering to others. The person of the catechist is the medium in which the message of the faith is incarnated. Whether catechists be parents, teachers, religious, priests, bishops, or any other of God's people, their witness to faith plays a pivotal role in catechesis.

National Catechetical Directory, Conclusion

Methods of Conditional Acceptance and Evaluation

The discussion about this roleplay centered on methods of conditional acceptance and evaluation of potential catechists. The first participant to comment about the roleplay said in this type of situation he would be very gracious in accepting the volunteer with the qualifying statement about reflection and updating that was made toward the end of the symposium roleplay. He would explain the recent developments in the life of the Church, and describe the process of catechesis as envisioned today. He wants the parishioner to feel welcomed. The participant said he makes sure that the parishioners who volunteer are aware of the renewal in liturgy and worship and other developments.

A second pastor offered another approach. In a similar situation he asked the volunteer: "What grade or what group would you like to teach?" He then had the parishioner sit in that class with the current catechist for a number of weeks, working with the catechist to become familiar with the process and procedures used with this grade level. In this example, the parishioner chose not to continue after six or eight weeks. He explained that he tries to encourage everyone who comes, but he insists that people have adequate time to make an informed decision about becoming a catechist.

Another pastor said he invites volunteers to participate in catechist formation programs before making a decision to become a catechist. He finds this process either transforms the person, or helps the person realize that catechesis is not the appropriate ministry for her or him. One priest explained that he invites volunteers to take a catechist's guide home to review. He later meets with them to share some experiences a catechist might encounter and to talk with them about ways to handle different situations. He explained that people who expect a clear direction often change their minds after reviewing the manual and learning what is expected.

Reflecting on this, a pastor expressed concern that people sometimes decide not to volunteer as catechists because they are given a manual to read and feel overwhelmed. He suggested that in small parishes, where catechist formation may not be available, mentoring may be the solution. The volunteer could be placed with someone who is a good catechist, and who could also be a companion. This process may help someone become a catechist who is not very familiar with this ministry.

NOTES

Two other pastors spoke about selection processes in their parishes that were similar. Once a year one parish gathers all the people interested in becoming a volunteer in one or more of the ministries of the parish. Members of the staff meet with them, screening them to see how their skills can best be used. Another parish gathers people together for study groups, and uses questionnaires to find out what model of the church each individual appears to embrace and how these models can fit together.

Reflection

How are catechists recruited, selected, and developed in your parish? What is done to give them a sense of empowerment?

"What Made Me the Priest I Am Today?"

During the evening meal some participants talked about the openness and acceptance that they observed at the symposium. As one person explained: "There's a certain attitude towards the Church. There's a certain acceptance of oneself that makes it possible to disagree at the table without becoming defensive." He said that although some pastors may approach catechesis and other ministries in different ways, the others still accept and affirm what is being done. Because of this, some participants thought it might be valuable for the group to talk about the factors that helped form them as priests. They thought that common experiences in formation may help explain why they are the way they are and why they empower catechetical ministry.

When this idea was proposed to the assembled participants, the group thought such an examination would be valuable. Therefore the symposium schedule was adjusted to accommodate this discussion. Each priest was asked to reflect upon "the most significant factors or influences that made you the priest you are today." After several minutes of reflection, the participants were asked to share their reflections at the table. After this sharing, each table summarized the insights and presented these to the group.

In their presentation, the priests at one table said that in looking for a common denominator, the one thing that clearly came across was the opportunity to expand themselves at the diocesan level, at the national level, and in some cases the international level. Going out of the diocese and being involved with other people opened up new avenues and helped them see things from a different perspective. In addition, all were involved in very long and important support groups that have shaped them through the years—with priests and with lay people. Their families also played an important role in their formation.

A priest at another table reported that: "We were very common. All of us were talking about the same things." There were three areas. The first was an openness to continuing formation, "our original formation and then the continuing formation especially since Vatican II." Next was the pursuit of continuing education. The third area was that of relationship. The participant said this was "something we were really delighted by. All of us spoke of the influence of women in our lives." He explained that this influence helped to shape them and made them more open to people and friendship.

The priests at another table also found a a common theme in relationships, especially those "that have helped to bring out the persons that we are." In addition, several said there were influenced by the era in which they developed. "We went through the seminary at the time of the Second Vatican Council, and much of what was going on the in the world and society in the 60's was quite formative for us. We had liberating experiences, experiences of overcoming, at one point, feelings of rigidity and then opening up to a great liberation. It was overcoming feelings of being indispensable and realizing that we are not the Messiah."

NOTES

NOTES

Another group reported that in their formation "there seemed to be a search for a meaning, a deeper meaning in life, especially in the areas where religion and life didn't seem to always mesh, and trying to find experiences where religion and life did. And trying to find a new paradigm and different ways of expressing that. Relationships also are very important in deepening. They call us forth." They also shared the perspective of trying to find a new way of doing things as "an adult on the journey."

The other priests shared similar experiences. They spoke of the importance of relationships in their formation, particularly with their families, close friends, and priest friends. Ongoing education was another key. Some spoke of coming to or leaving a foreign country, or moving to a different part of the country as a change, in terms of culture and church, that helped them grow. And some spoke of surviving crises and various events in life.

Reflection

What made you the priest/DRE/catechist you are today? How do these formative forces affect your catechetical ministry?

Catechetical Actions

At the end of the session, the participants were asked to identify specific activities they do with groups involved with catechetical ministry. The people at each table then compared and critiqued their lists to be sure the actions were specific and concrete. This also helped surface some different ideas.

Take some time now to think about and answer the following questions. A sample of responses by the participants appears at the end.

- What do you do catechetically with the total parish community?

- What do you do catechetically with the staff – your professional staff, your part time or full time staff?

- What do you do catechetically with the DRE?

- What do you do with the parish council, or the pastoral council?

NOTES

- What do you do with the education committee or the education commission?

- What do you do with catechists?

- What do you do with programs for adults catechetically?

- What do you do with programs for adolescents or youths catechetically?

- What do you do for programs for children catechetically?

- What do you do with parents catechetically?

- What do you do catechetically regarding budget?

- What do you do regarding catechesis with diocesan programs or services? Do you utilize them, do you ignore them, do you help pay for them?

- Is there anything else you do catechetically?

NOTES

> *Responses from the symposium participants*
>
> **Catechetical Actions:**
>
> **What do you do catechetically with the total parish community?**
> - Worship. This experience is crucial.
> - Prepare the best possible homilies, clarify the word, apply it to our lives.
> - Articulate a parish vision and work to follow it.
> - Provide bulletin articles and inserts.
> - Offer opportunities for catechetical involvement at all levels.
>
> **What do you do catechetically with the staff?**
> - Pray with them, study and reflect scripture, attend workshops and conferences.
> - Hold weekly staff meetings to plan and coordinate parish ministries.
> - Talk each week about our parish vision, how we can improve things together.
> - Give them authority in their responsibilities and affirm their decisions.
>
> **What do you do catechetically with the DRE?**
> - Pray together.
> - Meet a few times a week for formal and informal review of activities.
> - Provide personnel, facilities, and resources.
> - Support participation in workshops, seminars, and retreats.
> - Serve as resource person and sounding board for ideas.
>
> **What do you do with the parish council, or the pastoral council?**
> - Plan with them for adult catechesis.
> - Call them to follow the parish mission statement.
> - Update, pray, reflect.
> - Listen, support, challenge them to be living witnesses of the gospel.
> - Involve them in interviews with confirmation candidates.
>
> **What do you do with the education committee or commission?**
> - Insist on it being a Board for Total Faith Formation for all ages.
> - Listen to needs and plan a vision and strategy to address needs.
> - Hold monthly meetings to pray, study, evaluate, plan.
> - Encourage when struggling and praise for success.
> - Provide for enrichment through encouragement and financial assistance.
>
> **What do you do with catechists?**
> - Recruit, commission, and recognize; visit classes.
> - Encourage ongoing formation, provide financial support for training.
> - Affirm them personally and publicly.
> - Cook dinners for them.
> - Share common stories as we journey together.

Responses from the symposium participants

Catechetical Actions:

What do you do with programs for adults catechetically?
- Have adult education programs in Lent and Advent.
- Offer a parish retreat and a parish mission.
- Discern needs, provide programs, speakers.
- Teach scripture and morality series.
- Speak at meetings of traditional societies.

What do you do with programs for adolescents or youths?
- Provide and support a Youth Minister.
- Offer opportunities for ministry involvement.
- Have youth retreats in English and Spanish.
- Visit sessions and attend youth events.
- Encourage participation in diocesan leadership formation for youth.

What do you do for programs for children catechetically?
- Know their names and show how happy I am to see them coming.
- Have regular classes in religious education, school, and confirmation.
- Encourage and support with presence by visiting them regularly at class.
- Offer children's liturgies and homilies.
- Work with DRE and family centered religious education.

What do you do with parents catechetically?
- Take an active role in programs for parents.
- Give them resources to do sacramental preparation.
- Support parent formation with personal counseling.
- Hold personal interviews with parents of confirmation candidates.
- Listen and often make suggestions from a religious perspective.

What do you do catechetically regarding budget?
- Develop budget with DRE and staff.
- Set high budget priority for catechesis.
- Rely on volunteers because of a small budget.
- Find sufficient funds and get groups to support various projects.

What do you do with diocesan programs or services?
- Encourage participation in formation and pay for it.
- On occasion assist in formation or host it.
- Make catechists aware of what is available.
- Utilize Resource Center.
- Bring in diocesan staff to give workshops, retreats, etc.

Is there anything else you do catechetically?
- Encourage staff knowledge of all catechetical programs in the parish.
- Read, attend workshops, give workshops.
- Train evangelizers for neighborhoods for basic Christian communities.

NOTES

NOTES

Summary

All members of the Church are called to grow in faith and proclaim the Good News throughout their lives. Priests help members of the Church in their faith development and they also help their parishioners assume their roles in catechetical ministry and evangelization. The Spirit empowers. The priest is party to this empowerment.

Through discussion and through viewing and evaluating three roleplays, the participants further examined catechists and catechetical ministry. Several observations about the empowerment of people in catechetical ministry can be culled from these exercises.

- Sources of empowerment include:
    - Catechetical development of people in catechetical ministry
    - Personal development of people in catechetical ministry
    - Trust
    - Affirmation
    - Financial Support
    - Joy
    - Respect for time limitations
- A capable Director of Religious Education should have the responsibility and authority for the parish's catechetical program.
- Priests should be involved in the parish's catechetical programs to the extent that they are able to assist in providing direction as needed.
- Parents may need catechesis and motivation to accept their role in the catechesis of their children.
- To be part of a sacramental community, people must be willing to make commitments with regard to their faith.
- Pastors should view concerns of their staff as common concerns for the sake of the parish.
- Catechists should be recruited with care and experience opportunities for development through catechist formation or other programs.
- Some key components listed by the participants of their priestly development and formation include close and supportive relationships, continuing education and development, and ongoing formation.

The Next Step

The final segment examines and summarizes the insights that surfaced during the symposium. First, however, review your notes and reflections as well as the material in this chapter. In order to process this information, take some time and answer the questions on the following pages. Your responses can help you examine the role of the priest as empowerer of catechetical ministry in your parish. You can also use these responses as part of a broader planning segment at the end of the book.

■■ Planning Notes
■■ **The Priest as Empowerer of Catechetical Ministry**

What are your thoughts about empowerment?

In what ways does the priest empower catechetical ministry in your parish?

After reading the section on the empowerment of catechetical ministry, what may be areas of potential change or addition?

What are some resources for change—people, material, programs?

What are some obstacles or obstacles to change? How might you overcome them?

 Chapter 5
Conclusions

NOTES

Introduction

It is not only through the sacraments and the ministrations of the Church that the Holy Spirit makes holy the People, leads them and enriches them with his virtues. Allotting his gifts according as he wills (cf. 1 Corinthians 12:11), he also distributes special graces among the faithful of every rank. By these gifts he makes them fit and ready to undertake various tasks and offices for the renewal and building up of the church, as it is written, "the manifestation of the Spirit is given to everyone for profit" (1 Corinthians 12:7).

Lumen Gentium, 12

The symposium provided an opportunity to review the experiences and activities of priests who are effective in catechetical ministry. It did not start out with a specific list of points that must be followed for successful catechetical ministry, and it did not finish with one. During the concluding session the review of the events of the preceding days did not attempt to synthesize the discussions, enumerate key points, and hammer out a list of recommendations for empowering catechists and catechetical ministry.

During the concluding session, the participants were asked to record the insights from the symposium that they would share with different groups of people in catechetical ministry. They were also asked to record what they personally gained from the event. As throughout the symposium, the discussion that developed from these questions was marked by openness, honesty, and an exchange of good ideas as well as insights that came from approaches that had limited success.

In reviewing this information, it is helpful to think of a painting filled with colors and images. Specific details have a beauty unto themselves, but it is also necessary to step back and view the work as a whole. This advice applies not only to the chapter, but to the book as a whole. In other words, the specific activities are important, because they contribute to success. But taken together these activities contribute to a portrait of catechetical ministry in a parish. As in previous chapters, this chapter reports the discussion that took place. The concluding points at the end, however, are drawn from the entire symposium in order to provide a full portrait.

Synopsis

The final session began with the participants at each table sharing their responses to the question about empowerment on page 136. Table representatives then presented summaries of the table discussions to the entire group. The reports initiated additional discussion. Finally, the participants reflected on the insights they had gained from the symposium.

Before reading this chapter, please answer the following reflection question. If you wish, change a category if you believe another group of people would be more appropriate for you.

NOTES

Reflection

As a result of the symposium process, what would you say to the following groups about the priest's empowerment of catechetical ministry?

Catechists

Catechetical Leaders

Priests

Bishops

Empowerment Insights to Share

The responses to the question on the opposite page are grouped according to the following categories, and are not listed in order of priority. The participants often viewed the questions from a slightly different perspective, and so the reports taken together offer a full overall picture.

Catechists
- Crucial Ministry
- Growth and Development
- Affirmation
- Sharing
- Advice

Priests
- Crucial Ministry
- Growth and Development
- Work with Catechists

Catechetical Leaders
- Crucial Ministry
- Growth and Development
- Development of Catechists

Bishops
- Affirmation
- Support catechetical programs
- Develop Priests
- Provide Vision

Catechists

Crucial Ministry

The first speaker stated that his group would tell catechists that their ministry is vital to the life of the church, is united to the whole parish with the Sunday Eucharist, and is rooted in the ministry of the word. A priest at the table emphasized the importance of *telling* catechists their ministry is vital. These priests would also advise catechists to place greater emphasis on stewardship and discipleship.

Another group also would tell catechists that their work is essential to building the parish as a life-giving community of faith, grace, blessing, and service. In addition, they would say to the catechists: "*We* share in the work of sharing and living the gospel." Referring to this mutual responsibility, the pastor who was speaking for the others at the table explained that priests are catechists also, and priests have to identify with that. A priest from another group said the people at his table wanted to tell the catechists that "ministry is not just a task. It's formation and love for the church and love for who you are."

Growth and Development

One group would tell catechists that their ministry and witness are very important—they are ministers of the word called to inform, form, and transform Christians. Therefore, they should pray and strive to grow spiritually. To this end, priests should see if there are ways in which they can help catechists develop their faith, grow, and study. Catechists should be assured that they can count on their priests for support. The priests at another table also would recommend that catechists take advantage of continuing education and ongoing formation, attend workshops, and gather with other catechists. As one participant stated: "Continue to read, study, and grow to keep your own faith alive and your insights fresh when you share your faith with others."

Conclusions

NOTES

Affirmation

The reports emphasized the importance of affirming the catechists about the essential nature of their ministry—"they are the salt of the earth." One priest said it is important to tell catechists to enjoy what they are doing and not to be afraid, assuring them that they have been called to this ministry. Others said they would tell catechists to be confident and to utilize their unique gifts.

Sharing

The priests at one table would be sure to say that since the role of catechists is to invite others into the journey of life, catechists should share their journey of faith and listen to the stories of others. Another group, building on this point, would suggest that catechists pray and listen to their experiences, examine their own lives and make the connection between life issues and faith. Then in their ministry, they should allow communication to be a dialogue in which they listen to the experiences of others as they share their own. This interaction should include other catechists.

Advice

Several reports included some advice that the participants would share with the catechists. Catechists should bring parents along with the process. One priest stated that catechists should "support and encourage the adults. Show kindness and respect to the children. Tell your story of faith and listen to theirs. Pray." Another pastor would suggest that catechists include Christian service in their sessions because people learn by doing.

Catechetical Leaders

Crucial Ministry

One group of pastors said they would reiterate to catechetical leaders that catechesis is broader than the instruction that takes place in programs. Leaders should be involved in the wider dimension of the parish's programs, activities, and ministries, especially the social justice dimension, remembering that one important dimension of Christianity is demonstration. The priests would also encourage dialogue with pastors about catechesis.

Other priests said they would speak with catechetical leaders about the Rite of Christian Initiation of Adults as a model for formation, about ways in which catechesis can be presented to adults, and about the importance of Catholic identity. Another group of pastors said they also would speak about the priority of adult catechesis. In addition, the participants said they would share ideas with diocesan leaders, encourage them, and thank them for all they do.

Growth and Development

Praying with the leaders and catechists more frequently was another resolution. The priests would send parish catechetical leaders for additional training and urge the leaders to have greater interaction with the parish council. Participants also would encourage the parish leaders to stay abreast with current catechetical developments and to be open to new and creative approaches.

One priest explained that catechesis is a very intentional activity that demands people to know who they are and what they do. A group also spoke about the possibility of convening diocesan priests and DRE's for a one day symposium similar to the present one. The purpose would be to surface feelings from these people about the current experience and what direction they would like the diocese to take in catechetical ministry.

Catechist Development

The priests at one table would caution catechetical leaders about the need to respect the team's time and home life. Because of this, DRE's and other leaders need to find creative ways of finding time for catechist formation. In a similar vein, another group of priests would caution the leaders not to overextend themselves by becoming too involved in other parish ministries.

A participant said the priests at his table would speak about the need to support the needs of the people the leaders serve, and the mutual responsibility of the leaders and priests to form catechists. Another table would also encourage the leaders to work as a team with their priests in calling, training, and empowering catechists. The reporter spoke of the need to provide opportunities for spiritual and formational growth, and to call forth the prophet and artist in each person. Another priest encouraged the development of small faith sharing groups.

Priests

Crucial Ministry

"Priests must give priority to catechetical ministry because it is foundational to all other ministries." This view was reflected throughout the presentations. The priests would tell other priests that their role is essential to sharing the faith, and that they can be either an aid or an obstacle. They would advise priests to be attentive to the support they give to catechists and to be present to the catechetical program. In addition, they would encourage priests to teach in the parish's catechetical program, if possible, since they believe this is such an important aspect of parish life and ministry. Others said that if priests do not teach, they should have a direct involvement in the ministry of catechesis though their presence, support, and affirmation.

In reporting the consensus of his table, one priest stated: "We all got the feeling that the Church in the United States is alive and well." This group would remind priests that their preaching is their primary catechesis and that priests should make sure the parish has catechetical goals and realizes that catechesis is a shared responsibility of the entire Christian community. One pastor would suggest that the staff examine the question: "What is catechesis and how does it happen?"

Another group said priests should view themselves as servants, and they should love the people they serve. As expressed by one person: "You are modeling Christ. Be tender, compassionate, patient. Overlook much. Rejoice always. Pray."

NOTES

Growth and Development

The need for the continuing education of priests was stressed throughout the reports. One group suggested that an emphasis should be placed on sabbaticals. Another would advise priests to develop the skills of listening, learning, support, and empowerment. One table said they would tell priests to ask themselves: "What made me the priest that I am today?" A pastor observed that priests should remember that they are brothers, and that they can talk with one another. One pastor said: "We have to continue to pray for and with one another. We have to work together and support one another. Let us strive to practice and live what we preach. Let us listen to one another."

Work with Catechists

One pastor would tell his fellow priests: "We need to grow spiritually, in intimacy with Christ to empower our catechists and catechetical leaders and evangelizers." Other observations were that priests should be aware of their own strengths and weaknesses. They should use their best gifts and realize that they do not know it all and they can not do it all. In a community filled with gifts, the priest does not have to have each one. Priests should dialogue with the DRE's and come to a better understanding of the challenges that face them. They should serve as a good sounding board to the DRE and support the DRE, and they should be available to the catechists and work as a team. One pastor said his advice would be: "Nurture your catechists through ongoing affirmation, supporting their participation in courses, workshops, and other educational opportunities. Their ministry affects all the activities of the parish."

Bishops

Affirmation

One group said they would affirm the bishop and uphold his ministry because it is so difficult. Another table would encourage the bishop to continue to love the priests and work with them, be open to them and to what they may say. It is also important to trust and listen to all the people. Others would advise their bishop to be proud and confident of himself and of the priests of his diocese.

Support Parish Catechetical Programs

The priests in one group would urge their bishops to continue the course of strong catechetical programs in the parishes and to maintain a commitment to financial support for these catechetical programs. As one pastor explained: "We need to talk to him about the priority of catechesis in the life of our church." Priests at one table would recommend that the diocesan catechetical office be expanded to include regional offices with more staff on the road.

Others would point out to their bishops that parishes that give catechesis a priority are vibrant. One pastor explained that he would say: "Catechesis is more than teaching religion to children. Be especially concerned with the climate of faith that is being engendered in the entire parish. Parishes that give catechesis priority are alive and active in all ways. Look at the liturgies, the social outreach, the adult programs, the parent support. These indicate how effectively the parish is performing its catechetical ministry."

The participants would also urge the bishop to spend more time in the parishes because his involvement, support, and presence are important. Catechetical formation is crucial, and so they would ask the bishop to affirm the priests, catechetical leaders, and catechists who proclaim God's word. They would also suggest that the bishop encourage priests to be more effective catechetical leaders. One group of participants would also suggest that when a bishop visits a parish, he meet with catechists as well as with teachers, and with the DRE as well as with the school principal.

Develop Priests

Several table reporters said they would like to share the results of the symposium with their bishops to explore how these experiences can be applied. One pastor would encourage the bishop to continue to animate priests in their ongoing formation so they are better able to form evangelizers and to be catechetical guides and leaders who empower catechists for all ages. Some specific recommendations surfaced during the reports: bishops should help priests improve their homilies and liturgies; they should challenge priests to grow; and they should encourage sabbaticals.

Provide Vision

The consensus of one group was that the diocese must provide a clear vision of what is needed to be an active parish. To help accomplish this, the bishop should give vision and he should find someone he trusts to help pastors have a vision of what parishes should be doing. This group would also urge the bishop to encourage parishes to evangelize, to become an evangelizing community of communities. He should also encourage priests and catechetical leaders to work for a balanced approach to catechesis that integrates the discipleship nature of parish life with the formational aspects of programs.

Reflection

How can you apply some of these ideas to your parish? Can you add any of your own?

NOTES

Questions and Challenges

During the presentations, a participant wondered whether the symposium had come to grips with challenges facing the catechetical ministry of the church. His comments helped initiate a discussion covering these topics:

- Impediments to Catechesis
- Adult Catechesis
- A New Paradigm

Impediments to Catechesis

One pastor felt some major issues were not addressed at the symposium. Specifically, he referred to "the consumerism that blinds people to the message of God." He related the story in the gospel of Mark in which Jesus tells the young man to sell everything he has. "That story to me is what catechesis is about. I think Jesus is telling us that what our catechesis is meant to do is to promote that process of liberation, of surrender, of losing everything for the kingdom. Today we are so addicted, we are so attached that our society is yearning for a catechesis of detachment and freedom." He felt the discussions overlooked issues such as these impediments and instead focused on catechetical programs.

Another participant also expressed concern about the material temptations in society. "Those are the demons of our day that need to be dealt with before we ever do any catechizing." He believes that people have to realize that success as measured by society is not the life that the Lord offers. Until this happens, he thinks people are never going to be open enough to accept God's love in their lives and live in God's way and truth.

A fellow pastor did not agree that the symposium should have examined issues of this nature. "I would not begin by worrying about the demons in society. They exist for sure, but if we're going to take the demons on directly, we'll spend our time playing with the demons."

Need for Adult Level Catechetical Material

An additional area of concern was meeting the need for adult level catechetical material. One participant said that it is critical to work with adults and help them become disciples, and so pastors must expand their vision in that direction. He explained that many people return to the Church with a sketchy knowledge of it. Pastors and catechetical leaders are faced with the vast task of re-evangelizing adults and then enriching and deepening their Christian lives with a variety of topics, such as scripture study, marriage enrichment, and parenting classes. He said he has trouble obtaining appropriate material for these adult-centered ministries, and he thinks that pastors are going to have to pay much more attention to this in the future.

A New Paradigm?

Another issue was raised by a participant who thought the symposium should have articulated a new paradigm, a clear model for catechesis that addresses the need to change radically the catechetical setting. He believes that most parishes approach catechesis primarily from an educational perspective and so underemphasize or neglect the importance of the life-lived aspect of discipleship. In his view, catechesis at one time consisted primarily and almost exclusively of handing over information. "I'm suggesting it isn't working anymore. It might have at one time, but it isn't working. I don't think it will ever work again because that's not what we're about in terms of the goal we have."

He thinks that parishes can no longer rely on educational programs alone, whether these are parish religious education programs, Catholic School classes, or adult scripture study. He firmly believes that the parish community must be rooted in discipleship. He said the symposium contained many discussions about the positive dynamics of small groups, the growth of priests, and cultural experiences. However, he felt the discussions usually fell within the context of information, not relationship.

He told the participants they are successful catechists because "you by accident, by intention, or by the grace of God—all three of them probably—are in a discipleship mode in your life, in your lifestyle, in your mentality, and in your focus. That's why it works." He told them that reaching this position required courage and growth, but he added: "We need to look at a much more radical understanding of what it is that's going to change this nation if we're going to be helpful to recapturing our churches, our people and our faith."

The Educational Component

Several people offered observations. One participant explained that what drives him in his ministry is a similar vision of the Church that embraces a strong sense of discipleship, but catechesis needs to have good systems. "I think we have to be church. Church for us is being catholic, having an enormous diversity and unity, and is able to have many different models functioning, all of which are beneficial to the proclamation of the kingdom." He thinks the question must be to discern what works best in individual situations, and he doubts that anyone can create a radically new paradigm that will work for everyone. "I think if we all focus more on how we can be the church of Jesus Christ, and how we can bring the message of the gospel to our people, that's where we're going to begin to find the light. And that will involve all kinds of different models and gifts."

Referring to a discussion that the priests had about the forces that formed them, another participant said that education seemed to play a significant role in everyone's experience. He expressed his belief that education in all its facets helps shape people's attitudes, and to a large extent it was education that helped everyone in the room get to where they are today. He reiterated the belief that catechesis must be comprised of both discipleship and education. The goal is the same, but the means to achieve it is different. He sees it as a complex issue.

Conclusions

NOTES

Another pastor added: "I think even processes have to be programmed." He said that his parish's RCIA ministry has ninety catechumens a year. Formation on this scale requires a great deal of organization and could not be accomplished by process alone. He continued: "I agree with a lot of what is said as far as the most effective way of moving people is often one on one encounters, but I still speak in favor of some sense of organization to provide those types of opportunities. I don't think a textbook is a be all and end all, but what it does provide is an orderly curriculum for the catechist, a model for them to follow."

The Discipleship Component

Reflecting the need for greater emphasis on discipleship in many parishes, one participant explained that he no longer thinks that it is possible to hand on the faith. He then referred to a statement, quoted earlier in the symposium. The statement expressed the point for him that it is easier to act your way into a new way of thinking than think your way into a new way of acting. He explained: "If we want people to be faith-filled disciples of the Lord Jesus, *we've* got to be faith-filled disciples of the Lord Jesus, and other people will be attracted by that and we'll grow. If we can't do that, I don't think we can hand on the faith. If we do, we're handing on information, we're handing on knowledge, but it may not change people's lives."

Citing the role of service in catechesis and the pressure on young people to conform to consumerist values of society, another participant spoke about one family's catechetical experience. Members of a family helped distribute blankets collected by their suburban parish for the homeless in the city. The parents involved one of their teenaged sons in this effort, which required them to be on a train at 6:30 in the morning. The project turned out to be a great catechetical moment of growth for the entire family. Referring to this, the participant said it is important to talk about what people do, and not only what they do not or should not do.

A participant reflected that catechetical ministry as envisioned by the Church and its documents is an effort at discipleship. Catechesis is an integration of message, worship, community and service. It is making faith become living, conscious and active in the life of a person, and that is discipleship. He said if any question arises between what is catechesis and what is discipleship, then it is necessary to look sincerely at the ways catechesis is approached to see if this is faithful to what people have been called to by the Church. He thinks the problem surfaces when catechesis is limited to an instructional model that emphasizes message without commensurate attention to community, worship, and service. "So maybe if we were called back to how the Church has already presented catechesis to us, we would be implementing a discipleship model."

Another priest said he did not hear a challenge for great change, but rather a call to look at outcomes. He feels that contemporary catechesis *is* different and that it *is* changing the Church. An invitation to families to take priority time to sit down and do some catechetical moments in their own experience is changing the priorities of family life. An invitation to adults to sit in a small group and talk with each other about their struggle to believe and understand their struggle differs from the American notion of 'hang in there and do it by yourself.' He thinks catechists should tell people: "We're asking you to do something that's different, challenging and costly, but because you're going to do it, we're going to change."

Trust the Holy Spirit

A participant said that for him, priesthood meant walking away from what he considered for a time to be everything that was important in this world. That changed his life tremendously. He said he had to step into mystery, he had to really step into darkness. Becoming a priest required choices and decisions, leaving behind attitudes, paradigms, and models of the church.

He thinks the whole Church did the same thing after the Second Vatican Council, and so the Church is experiencing the same type of mystery as when he took his leap of faith. "We're like the parable of the seed planted, where the farmers perhaps have gone to bed and gotten up the next day and looked out the window and there's nothing there. And that's what it is and that's what it feels like and I think we just need to know that. But to know that we are on the way."

Another priest recalled the years following his ordination during which much of his time was devoted to the renovation of the parish church and school buildings. At the time, he privately questioned these efforts. However, after he left, the demographics of the neighborhood changed drastically and many buildings in the area burned down or were abandoned. The one symbol that remained was the parish plant, the church building and the school. The school, because it was in excellent condition, was able to be used to educate the people coming into the area. Helped by the efforts of the parish, the people eventually rebuilt that whole neighborhood. Looking back, he reflected how one may not appreciate what one is doing. "So you let the Spirit work through you. You do the best you can and sometimes you're successful, sometimes you're not."

A fellow pastor offered a similar observation after listening to the discussions. "The thing that I hear is that we simply witness the faith that we have and we proclaim the kingdom in the midst of all this confusion, and the rest I guess belongs to God. Maybe we just have to be humble enough to accept that."

Conclusions

NOTES

Reflection

During their discussions, the participants were asked to pause for a few minutes to respond to the following questions. Before you continue, please use these questions to think about insights you may have gained from this material. Responses from the participants appear on the following pages.

- What has this experience meant to you personally?

- What does this experience mean for your ministry?

- I now see that I empower catechetical ministry most effectively by:

Responses from the symposium participants

What has this experience meant to you personally?

- I have been energized by interacting with pastors who are excited about their ministry who have a healthy vision of Church, who are secure in themselves.

- It has been a humbling experience and an invigorating experience. I had to rethink and clarify in my own mind certain concepts, vocabulary, etc., and reflect on what I am doing and how I come to have the vision I have of Church and people. I love people and people are the Church.

- It has been invigorating. I gained valued insights from the discussions and a great understanding and consciousness of the meaning of catechesis—how broad it is.

- Very uplifting. It helped me to get in touch with some very creative and dedicated priests. Helps give one a more solid basis on which to speak about effective catechesis in parishes and the kind of leadership needed.

- A great experience of being with and sharing with a group of people who are struggling with living the message of empowerment and discipleship. A sense of *sympatico*.

- It has energized me to know that other priests are working towards a similar view of Church: adult faith centered, energized, committed Christians. It has exhausted me thinking that much of our work of genuine catechesis is still to be done—bringing about true conversion and evangelization in the lives of Catholic Christians.

- It validated my conviction that <u>everyone</u> has a piece of the Good News, and the Truth that is in it. No <u>one</u> has it all, and that's OK.

- It has affirmed that the empowering process is going in my life without my really realizing it was going on.

- Great awareness of struggles in catechetical ministry. Very common struggles. How to effectively catechize as people? Every part of the country is so different in terms of needs, expectations and challenges to helping people on the journey of faith.

- We are people who have the same goals in ministry but have become more and more aware that we view the means to achieve these goals differently—sort of a microcosm of our experience as Church.

- I have grown personally by hearing many effective efforts done in other parishes. I have benefited by meeting priests from throughout the U.S. who have much greater experiences and learned from that.

- This experience has enlivened my faith and priesthood. It has challenged me to continue to be open.

<u>NOTES</u>

Conclusions

NOTES

> *Responses from the symposium participants*
>
> **What has this experience meant for your ministry?**
>
> - Be open. Listen, truly listen to others.
>
> - I have reviewed my thoughts regarding catechesis. I have been reinforced in my ministry of catechesis.
>
> - What I have heard has affected what I am doing. At the same time it has given me the chance to look at my ministry in a different light. I have learned from others ways I can improve what is happening in my parish. I'm not discouraged by our parish's shortcomings, for we all have them.
>
> - For my ministry, I plan on meeting with our Diocesan Director to share with him my experience and to see where we go from here in the diocese and in the parish. I have seen areas where I need to give more emphasis.
>
> - There is a willingness to go back to support the work of catechesis more vocally and consciously.
>
> - I will be more intentional in promoting and enabling catechetical ministry for all in the parish. Most especially, I will be more affirming and supportive of our catechetical leaders.
>
> - I will approach my ministry with some fresh perspective and renewed enthusiasm.
>
> - It means I am more confident in my approach and style of leadership with others. It means I realize more than ever the importance of life-giving relationships in my life.
>
> - I will be looking for ways to enhance adult catechesis, rather than to limit focus on children, adolescents, and pre-sacrament programs for parents.
>
> - I see the parish as a whole community and I am one with them. Programs, etc., are developed in and through the community.
>
> - I have a desire to talk with others about catechesis.
>
> - There is new energy to stay with the struggle of evangelization of people, and new energy to do more reflection on my own spirituality and my responsibility to live as a disciple of the Lord.
>
> - I will be more proactive in helping to determine the direction our parish needs to take.
>
> - My ministry will change direction in the area of catechesis. I need to develop stronger adult education opportunities in my parish.
>
> - This experience affirms my ministry, tells me to do more of what I do, and to listen more and pray more.

Responses from the symposium participants

I now see that I empower catechetical ministry most effectively by:

- Sharing what I have been gifted with.

- Supporting and recognizing and receiving catechists as professionals who care about their work and the results it produces.

- Really living out of the fact that the Church is a community and together we make up an organic whole. We are the image of God!

- Affirming, being present, providing vision.

- Letting go. Visiting people, getting to know them, making it easy and comfortable for them to volunteer on a limited time basis and to step down with dignity and a sense of accomplishment. A lot of people doing a little, rather than few doing a lot.

- I am most effective because of the way I treat people, the way I celebrate liturgy, and the way I live. I believe that comes from my prayer, my communion with the Lord, and relationships with others.

- Bringing and sharing a vision and helping catechists grow through modeling, support, and affirmation.

- My vision of the Church, my dedication to forming such Church in the parish, and by being a model for others in ministry.

- By direct involvement in catechetical ministry—presence, support, affirmation.

- In my leadership role as pastor I need to affirm the faith, proclaim it, experience God's grace in me so that I can effectively speak, act, challenge, name, convert— and stand in midst of community as priest.

- Being more authentically myself and continuing to do what I am doing. (I also need to be more tuned into our catechists.)

- Most effectively, by preaching. Also, I empower by walking with catechists, by challenging catechists and parishioners to ask deeper questions of life, and to see the Lord in that.

- I now see that I empower catechists most effectively by my passion for what I see is the heart and soul of the good news.

- I empower catechists more effectively by coming to know them better, listening, affirming them, helping them to grow spiritually and to live as disciples of Christ.

- To the degree that I am open to conversion, dialogue, challenge, presence and loving, I give witness to the Lord we walk with together.

- Helping catechists and parents work as partners in catechesis. We are one family and Church in the name of Jesus.

NOTES

Conclusions

NOTES

Conclusion

The information from the symposium does not provide a definitive answer to the presentation of catechesis or the empowerment of catechetical ministry. As a pastor observed during the final discussion, there is no single approach to catechetical ministry for parishes throughout the country. However, based on the experience of the pastors who participated, the material does provide valuable guidelines to follow.

The symposium identified many elements which are present when priests help empower those who serve in catechetical ministry. The Holy Spirit is the true empowerer, but the participants nurture and predispose the people to the power of the Spirit. The empowerment of catechists and catechetical ministry flows naturally from the dedication of the priests to catechetical ministry as well as from their approach to it—catechesis finds expression through message, community, worship, and service. The participants believe that priests must give priority to catechetical ministry because it is foundational to all other ministries.

Thankful for their strengths and aware of their weaknesses, the participants are secure individuals who are not threatened by the successes of others. They realize that they do not possess all the skills and knowledge needed to run a parish, and that the work of the Lord must be spread among all the people of God. The participants recognize the talents of others, they encourage parishioners to use these talents, and they provide opportunities for spiritual formation, enrichment, and ongoing leadership development. They also give confidence through trust. This is true not only in the areas that are specifically catechetical, but in a wide array of ministries.

The body of information in this chapter and the preceding ones records responses from exercises and discussions in which the participants review their experiences in the areas of parish, catechesis in the parish, the priest in catechetical ministry, and the priest as empowerer of catechetical ministry. In addition, the book puts the responses into a larger focus, processing them and placing them in the context of Church documents. This juxtaposition helps illustrate how the approaches of the participants support the teaching of the Church. As one of the participants observed: "It is necessary to sincerely look at the ways catechesis is approached to see if this is faithful to what we have been called to by the Church."

The next four pages recap the key points that were made in each area of the symposium. The information gleaned from the symposium provides excellent guidance, but you and the others involved in your parish's catechetical ministry must also examine your experience. More than likely, you have many helpful ideas, insights, and experiences of your own. Throughout the chapters you were asked to reflect on your parish's experience in catechetical ministry as well as that of the participants. Based on this, you could then consider aspects of ministry in your parish that might need to be strengthened or improved. Use the next chapter to help you and your parish articulate those ideas and design a plan to achieve the goals desired in catechetical ministry.

The Parish: Summary Points

- The parishes provide the environment in which the people of God can come together as a community of faith.

- The vigor and vision of the parish depend on several factors, but should always be focused on the Church's mission of catechesis and evangelization.

- The parishes demonstrate a strong discipleship model. Pastors develop lay leaders and empower them to make parish ministries their own.

- The parishes display a strong sense of stewardship. Parishioners apply their time, skills, and money to serve God and neighbor, providing witness to the tenets of Christianity. These works embrace parishioners and non-parishioners, at times supplementing services provided by government. Absence of the parish would deprive the neighboring community not only of service, but of significant moral leadership.

- The parishes seek to increase awareness and involvement in national issues.

- Many parishes actively participate in service to the global community. More than half have a twinning relationship with a parish in another country.

- The pastors work with and help the laity to grow in faith. A critical avenue for this is the Sunday liturgy which includes a well-prepared homily.

- Bishops should encourage parishes to evangelize, to become an evangelizing community of communities. They should also encourage priests and catechetical leaders to work for a balanced approach to catechesis that integrates the discipleship nature of parish life with the educational and formational aspects of programs.

Reflection

What attributes from this list or your own ministerial experience need more emphasis in your parish? How might your parish do this?

Conclusions

NOTES

Catechesis in the Parish: Summary Points

- All members of the church community are called to develop and strengthen their loving relationship with God throughout their lifetime. They are also called to help others do the same.

- Catechesis is an ongoing faith formation that should occur from cradle to tomb. The foundation is rooted in family and childhood, but catechesis continues through adolescence and into adulthood. Being capable of a mature faith, adults have the responsibility for ongoing spiritual growth.

- Catechesis begins and continues in the home, supported and complemented by parish programs for all age levels.

- Catechesis is intergenerationally supportive. All people within the family, and within the parish, can aid the faith formation of the other members— children, youth, adults, and the elderly.

- The ministry of the word is essential to a strong faith. Homilies must be prepared carefully and be appropriate to the faithful.

- Catechesis is not a separate component that occurs at designated times. The ongoing development and discernment of faith takes place in all activities and responsibility falls on all members of the parish to catechize and evangelize.

- Priests should affirm catechists, acknowledging their ministry as vital to the life of the church, united to the whole parish with the Sunday Eucharist, and rooted in the ministry of the word. They should encourage them to enjoy what they are doing and not to be afraid, be confident and to utilize their unique gifts. Priests should also assure catechists that they have been called to this ministry.

- Catechists should pray and strive to grow spiritually. They should take advantage of continuing education and ongoing formation, attend workshops, and gather with other catechists.

- Catechetical leaders should be involved in the wider dimension of the parish's programs, activities, and ministries, especially the social justice dimension.

Reflection

What might you or your parish do to enrich your parish's catechetical ministry?

The Priest in Catechetical Ministry: Summary Points

- Priests must give priority to catechetical ministry because it is foundational to all other ministries.

- The importance of the word, of preaching well-prepared homilies as part of well-planned liturgical celebrations, is a critical factor in the priest's role in catechetical ministry.

- The participants' approach to catechesis has education and discipleship in a synergistic balance. Religious education comprises only one component of catechesis in the parish. Although the participants participate in catechetical programs, they make sure that others are prepared and capable to handle these responsibilities.

- The participants recognize that they cannot do everything and so they do not place excessive expectations on themselves. They are secure people. They are comfortable with having parishioners with complementary talents work with them, and so they actively develop lay ministry.

- The participants nurture the faith of parishioners and help them pass this faith to others. So parishioners can accomplish their catechetical mission, the priests help them recognize, develop, and use their God-given talents.

- In providing leadership, the participants help the parish develop a vision of catechesis, help the parish to focus on this vision, and then focus the talents of the people to help the parish carry this vision.

- The participants see that most of their ministry entails catechesis. Since there are opportunities for catechesis in so much of what the priests do, an important aspect of the catechetical role of priests is being present to people, talking and listening to them.

- Priests should pray with catechists and catechetical leaders more frequently. They should see if there are ways in which they can help catechists develop their faith, grow, and study.

- If priests do not teach in a program, they should have direct involvement in the ministry of catechesis though their presence, support, and affirmation.

- Bishops should continue to encourage priests in their ongoing formation so the priests are better able to form evangelizers and to be catechetical guides and leaders who empower catechists for all ages. They should help priests improve their homilies and liturgies; they should challenge priests to grow; and they should encourage sabbaticals.

Reflection

In your parish, what might a priest do to enrich the parish's catechetical agenda?

Conclusions

NOTES

The Priest as Empowerer of Catechetical Ministry: Summary Points

- All members of the Church are called to grow in faith and proclaim the Good News throughout their lives.
- The priests nurture the spiritual growth of parishioners and they help parishioners assume their roles in catechetical ministry and evangelization.
- The Spirit empowers. The priest is party to this empowerment.
- Sources of empowerment include:
  - Catechetical development of people in catechetical ministry
  - Personal development of people in catechetical ministry
  - Trust
  - Affirmation
  - Financial Support
  - Joy
  - Respect for time limitations
- A capable Director of Religious Education should have the responsibility for developing and administering the parish's catechetical programs.
- Priests should know about the parish's catechetical programs and be able to provide direction as needed.
- Catechists should be recruited with care and experience opportunities for development through catechist formation or other programs.

Reflection

What might be done in your parish to enhance the empowerment of catechists and catechetical ministry?

Chapter 6
Creating Action Plans

NOTES

Introduction

Do not think lightly of any advice that can be useful. At all times bless the Lord God, and ask him to make all your paths straight and to grant success to all your endeavors and plans.

Tobit 4:18–19

In order to assist the catechetical ministry of others, a group of priests who are successful in catechetical ministry shared their insights and experiences during a three day symposium. As you read about the discussions they had about the parish, catechesis in the parish, the priest in catechetical ministry, and the priest as empowerer of catechetical ministry, you were asked to think about your own experience in catechetical ministry and to compare it with that of the participants. You may have identified areas of possible change, improvement, or further exploration, and at the end of each chapter you had the opportunity to develop ideas about potential change. Subsequent chapters may have influenced your thinking some more.

The goals you have may vary widely in scope. For example, one area of change may be personal—perhaps you want Sunday homilies to have more focus. However, another area may be more extensive—perhaps you would like to expand adult catechesis in the parish. Whatever your goal may be, if you want to accomplish it you must develop a plan.

A goal without a plan is merely wishful thinking.

You may have read this book on your own or as part of a larger group process such as parish staff enrichment, a diocesan workshop, or a day of recollection. No matter what the setting, if you have read the material and completed the exercises you have already committed substantial time and thought to this process. Do not stop now. If you have gained some insights, apply them. Working with the people in your parish, you can follow the planning process in this chapter or use an existing process or approach.

Creating Action Plans

As the first step in creating your Action Plans, list each dimension that you think calls for change or implementation. After reviewing this list, assign a priority to each item. As you know, you cannot accomplish everything at once. To develop plans for dimensions with the highest priority (not necessarily the ones that are easiest to accomplish), you can follow these steps:

- Set the goal for implementing change.
- Outline the steps needed to reach this goal.
- Identify resources for each step.
- Identify obstacles for each step.
- Identify solutions for the obstacles.
- Establish timeframes for each step.
- Assess progress and set dates for review.

Creating Action Plans

NOTES

Action Plan Components

Each component of the Action Plan is described below, and a sample of a completed plan appears on pages 158–160. Following the sample, there are two blank Actions Plans for your use beginning on page 161.

- *Goal.* What do you want to accomplish?

    The goal you set should be attainable. In relation to a three hour movie, the goal should be equivalent to one scene. Your goal must be realistic. It is not realistic to plan to implement a Lenten reflection program if the program has yet to be developed and Ash Wednesday is next week.

    Your goal should be specific. Reading it, a person should know exactly what you want to accomplish.

    The goal should be specific enough to be measured, even though the measurement may be subjective. For example, if a priest asks a group of parishioners to critique his homilies, the information he receives may be colored by opinion. However, he can offer the people some guidelines to help them focus on particular areas.

    Your goal should incorporate a time element. When do you want to reach this goal?

    Example: For Lent of next year the parish will have a small group faith sharing program with a target participation of two hundred people.

- *Steps.* What steps must be taken to attain this goal?

    List all the steps you think are needed to achieve your goal. Each step should be as specific as possible. You should describe the activity required, identify the person responsible for the activity, establish when the activity will be accomplished, and explain how the accomplishment of each step can be measured.

    Once you complete the list, number the items according to their sequence in time.

- *Resources.* Who can help you? What material can you use?

    Who are the people who can help you achieve this goal? Do these people have the knowledge and skills required to accomplish the tasks? If not, what type of development do they need?

    What are the physical resources that are needed to achieve this goal? These may include material such as *The Priest as Empowerer of Catechetical Ministry*, equipment, expenses, programs, and outside assistance.

- *Obstacles.* What obstacles may you encounter as you implement your plans? How can you avoid or overcome these obstacles?

  Think of the obstacles that may hinder the accomplishment of each step. These may include time, the availability of people, a specific situation, or the philosophical or catechetical outlook of the parish.

  What internal obstacles may be present? For example, there may be something you have wanted to achieve, but over the years you have put off action because of a personal reluctance.

- *Solutions.* For each of the obstacles listed, think of ways in which you can address them so they are no longer obstacles.

- *Timeframes.* How much time will be required to implement your plan?

  How long will it take between the initiation of the plan and its completion? Each step should have approximate timeframes.

- *Assessment.* How will you assess your progress? What checkpoints or measures should you use?

  Establish dates and measurements to review progress.

Reality Test

After drafting an action plan, it helps to have a person or a group of people review it. A person reviewing the plan may suggest something you overlooked, spot a flaw, or offer alternative approaches. This is an important step that you should not overlook.

Sample ACTION PLAN – page 1

Goal

What do you want to accomplish?

For Lent of next year the parish will have a small group faith sharing program with participation of 200 people.

Steps

What steps must be taken to attain this goal?

1. DRE and pastor to identify and invite people to be responsible for program.

2. Committee to decide to:
   a. acquire and use existing program, or
   b. develop a new program

   Some areas of consideration include approach, topics, structure, material needed, personnel required, cost and budget.

3. If decision is to develop a new program, interim development deadlines must be established.

4. The program must be ready by December 1. Begin plans for promotion and recruiting volunteers and participants.

5. Begin to promote program in early January.

6. Plans for training small group leaders should be completed during January.

7. People needed to lead small groups. Solicit volunteers in early January. All positions should be filled by the end of January.

8. Recruit and register participants at the end of January.

9. Begin training for small group leaders at the beginning of February.

10. Inaugurate program the Sunday before Ash Wednesday.

Sample ACTION PLAN – page 2

Resources

Who can help you? What material can you use?

People

- *potential committee members:*
  Jim and Gloria Mullen, Hank Garcia, Mary Nicholas, Lee Maxon, Grace Edwards . . .
  Brainstorm with DRE to think of people who are not too involved in other activities at present.
- *Speak with Pat Trager in the diocesan office.*

Material

- *diocesan office*
- *Review program used by St. John's parish.*

Obstacles

What obstacles may your group encounter as you implement your plans? How can you avoid or overcome these obstacles?

Obstacles: *Solutions:*

First time small group sharing in parish

• *Unfamiliarity*	• *familiarize through homily, bulletin, handouts' catechetical programs, etc.*
• *people don't think they need it*	• *stress ongoing development*
• *people lack time*	• *stress limited time required*
• *coordinators lack time*	• *material should require minimal preparation; limit time requirements for training, etc.*

Creating Action Plans

Sample ACTION PLAN – page 3

Timeframes

How much time will be required to implement your plans?

- *Form committee by July 1.*
- *Select approach by September 1.*
- *Have program ready by December 1.*
- *Complete training plans for small group leaders by January 1.*
- *Have promotion plans ready by January 1.*
- *Begin to promote second Sunday in January.*
- *All group leaders in place by January 31.*
- *Group leader training during first week in February.*
- *Inaugurate program the Sunday before Ash Wednesday.*

Assessment

How will you assess progress as the plan is implemented? What checkpoints or measures should you use?

- *Committee will monitor timeframes.*
- *Identify people who can review the material as it is developed (for training, program, etc.)*
- *Ask participants and group leaders for their evaluation and suggestions at the end of the program.*

ACTION PLAN – page 1

Goal

What do you want to accomplish?

Steps

What steps must be taken to attain this goal?

ACTION PLAN – page 2

Resources

Who can help you? What material can you use?

Obstacles

What obstacles may you encounter as you implement your plans? How can you avoid or overcome these obstacles?

Obstacles: Solutions:

ACTION PLAN – page 3

Timeframes

How much time will be required to implement your plans?

Assessment

How will you assess your progress? What checkpoints or measures should you use?

ACTION PLAN – page 1

Goal

What do you want to accomplish?

Steps

What steps must be taken to attain this goal?

ACTION PLAN – page 2

Resources

Who can help you? What material can you use?

Obstacles

What obstacles may you encounter as you implement your plans? How can you avoid or overcome these obstacles?

Obstacles: Solutions:

ACTION PLAN – page 3

Timeframes

How much time will be required to implement your plans?

Assessment

How will you assess your progress? What checkpoints or measures should you use?

 **Chapter 7**
The Symposium Process

Introduction

This book provides an opportunity to review the catechetical experiences of the priests who attended the symposium. However, you can also use it and the symposium process with a group of people to explore these insights, as well as the group's insights, about the empowerment of catechists and catechetical ministry. The process designed for the symposium can be adapted for a variety of settings. This chapter reviews how you can do this.

Potential Settings

- catechetical committee meetings
- *Catechism of the Catholic Church* planning days
- days of recollection
- deanery meetings
- diocesan workshops
- inservice days
- parish ministries workshops
- retreats
- seminars
- staff meetings

Possible Timeframes

- ½ day
- 1 day
- 3 days
- 2 hours of a meeting
- time spread over a period of weeks or months, e.g., ninety minutes of the second staff meeting of the month for four months

Approaches

Although this book provides a comprehensive summary of the symposium, take a few moments to review the detailed agenda on pages 171 to 175. This will give you a good overview of the components of the symposium as well as the time allocated for their completion.

As you can see from the detailed agenda, the symposium process has a modular structure with six distinct components that you can adapt according to your needs.

- Introduction
- The Parish
- Catechesis in the Parish
- The Priest in Catechetical Ministry
- The Priest as Empowerer of Catechetical Ministry
- Conclusion

The process can be adapted to fit many situations. However, if you want to plan a meeting for a group to examine catechetical ministry based on the symposium, formulating an agenda should be the last step in your planning process.

NOTES

Altogether, there are four steps you should follow:

- Identify your goal.
- Identify the people to be involved in this process.
- Determine the amount of time that will be available.
- Adapt the process to fit your goal, the people and the time, or modify your goal.

Your agenda depends on the variables in the first three steps. What do you want to accomplish as your goal? This may mean you focus on certain areas of the symposium. Who will attend? How many people will take part? What are the background and experience of the people? The number of people and their experience will affect the time allocated for exercises and discussion. How much time will be devoted to the meeting? Will there be adequate time to explore the topics? Once you consider these questions, ask whether or not you can accomplish your initial goal. If you do not think you can, then you should modify your goal.

Here is an example:

- You and your staff have a goal to foster a greater sense of catechetical mission in the activities of the parish.
- To help accomplish this, you want to involve the members of the parish pastoral council, since they are leaders and are active in many of the ministries of the parish.
- Because of the schedules of the members of the pastoral council, time is limited. However, there is a Saturday day of recollection scheduled for the fall and the spring. You and your staff feel that one of those two days could be dedicated for this type of formation process.
- In designing an agenda for a day long meeting to accomplish your goal, you decide to concentrate on two segments of the symposium: "Catechesis in the Parish" and "The Priest in Catechetical Ministry."

Working with the Agenda

Once you have identified the first three steps, you can begin to design your agenda using the following parts of the detailed agenda for the symposium.

Introduction

An introduction will be necessary, although the time allocated for this may vary significantly. During the introduction you will explain the purpose of the gathering, state your goal, and briefly describe what the participants will be doing. This will also give the participants an opportunity to introduce themselves to one another if necessary. These personal introductions should include some background information, for example, where the person comes from and what background or experience he or she has in catechetical ministry.

The Four Components

The approach to each segment of the symposium can be adapted according to your needs. The primary goal for each of these segments is to surface experiences and ideas that can be used to encourage the empowerment of catechists and catechetical ministry. The exercises used in the symposium were creative and effective. However, the number of people participating in the meeting you develop and the setting for the meeting may not be conducive to conducting some of the exercises as they are proposed here. Please use your own creativity to design something that will achieve the same end.

Before coming to the meeting, the participants should complete the reflection questions that begin the chapter being examined. As with the symposium, this will provide a reservoir of responses from which to draw. You may also want the participants to read the entire chapter before you meet. The benefits for this would be their exposure to ideas of others, which in turn may generate their own. The drawbacks would be that they may be influenced or inhibited.

Conclusion

As with an introduction, a conclusion will be important in any process that you design. During the conclusion the group should review its discussions, list the key issues that were identified, and examine how these issues can affect their catechetical ministry.

Resources

There are limited personnel and material needs for a meeting of this sort. The one person that the process truly requires is a facilitator.

Facilitator

The facilitator should be someone who can lead the discussion without dominating it. Ideally, the person should maintain a fairly neutral stance. However, with smaller groups, such as a parish staff, the facilitator will likely be an active participant in the discussion. As the leader of the process, the facilitator has overall responsibility for the meeting, and so should be certain that everything is in order and all the material is in place, etc.

Material

The material required depends to a certain extent on the facilities and on the number of people attending. However, the facilitator will need a flipchart and a set of colored markers to record the key points of the discussion. Each participant should have:

- pad and pen
- agenda
- statement of purpose
- name tag
- table name card
- *The Priest as Empowerer of Catechetical Ministry*

Optional items, such as copies of articles or other handouts, will depend upon the needs and background of the participants.

NOTES

If the number of people attending the meeting requires division into smaller groups for discussion, (with a minimum of four and a maximum of eight per table), then each of these groups should have marker and a flipchart or some means for recording the key points that are made. If possible, the participants should be seated at round tables to facilitate discussion.

The optimum number of people depends on the interaction that is possible among the participants and between the participants and the facilitator. Time is also a factor. For example, based on the number of small groups required for the anticipated number of people, how much time would be needed to listen to the table summaries required by some of the exercises?

Trust the Holy Spirit

Come, Holy Spirit, fill the hearts of Your faithful and enkindle in them the fire of Your love. Send forth Your Spirit and they shall be created. And You shall renew the face of the earth.

Whether you use this process in its entirety, adapt it, or design one of your own, do not fear. Be creative and use your talents to help empower catechists and catechetical ministry. Trust that the Holy Spirit supports your work in catechetical ministry.

The Symposium Process

The Priest as Empowerer of Catechetical Ministry
The Symposium Process—Detailed Agenda

                                                     Approximate
                                                    Time Allocation

DAY ONE

Arrival, Informal Gathering, and Recreation

DAY TWO

8:00 a.m.   Breakfast

8:45 a.m.   **Opening of Symposium**

Handout   Folders (at each place)
- Statement of Purpose   *[Handout 1]*
- Brief Agenda   *[Handout 2]*
- Name tags

        Introductions

- Welcome   (10)
  - History: How Symposium came about
           How participants were selected
  - Introduction of facilitators
  - Participants introduce themselves   (35)
    - Who they are
    - Where they are from
    - Experience in catechetical ministry

        Opening Prayer   (20)

        Brief Break   (05)

10:00 a.m.   **Intended Outcomes of Symposium**   (05)

- To identify elements needed for parish priests
  to empower those who serve in catechetical ministry
- To identify concrete ways of helping and supporting
  parish priests in their empowering ministry

10:05 a.m.   **Impact of the Parish**

- Table Discussions   (55)
  - What difference does your parish make on the lives
    of parishioners, the community, and national or global society?
  - Summarize notes for upcoming panel.
  - Each table selects one person for the panel to present
    the table summary to the group.

11:00 a.m.   Break   (15)

11:15 a.m.   **Impact of the Parish** (continued)

- Panel Discussions   (1:45)
  - Panel Reports
  - General Discussion
  - Reaction

The Symposium Process

                                                                           Approximate
                                                                          Time Allocation

DAY TWO (continued)

- 1:00 p.m.   Lunch

   (Afternoon Free)

- 5:15 p.m.   Hospitality

- 6:00 p.m.   Dinner

- 7:00 p.m.   **Catechesis in the Parish**

    - Overview of Topic   (20)
        - Relation between catechesis, parish mission, and ministries
        - Role and responsibilities of parish and family regarding catechesis
        - Large group brainstorming ("word bank") – facilitators use flipcharts to record participants' responses to the question: "What are some words or phrases that describe how you perceive catechesis?"
    - Table Discussions: (30)
        - In your parish, how do you see catechesis having an impact on the following areas?
            - mission
            - other parish ministries
            - parishioners
        - In your parish, how do you see the community carrying out its catechetical role?

- 7:50 p.m.   Brief Break   (10)

- 8:00 p.m.   **Catechesis in the Parish** (continued)

    - Table Discussions: (20)
        - Continued examination of both questions
        - Newsprint summaries of both questions
        - Each table appoints a spokesperson to report to the group.
    - Table Reports   (20)
    (This is done in place at the table, using the flipchart.)
    - General Discussion   (35)
        - What have we learned?
        - What patterns are emerging?

   Homework:
   Participants are asked to draw an image/symbol/picture that describes the priest's role in catechetical ministry for the morning session. They are to bring it to the session in the morning.

- 9:15 p.m.   **Closing Prayer**

- 9:30 p.m.   Hospitality

The Symposium Process

Approximate
Time Allocation

DAY THREE

8:00 a.m.   Breakfast

8:45 a.m.   **Morning Prayer**

9:00 a.m.   **The Priest in Catechetical Ministry**

- Table Discussions   (90)
    - Share homework images.
    - Create a table image/collage of priest's role in catechetical ministry. (flipcharts)
    - Share table images with entire group.
    - Discuss challenges inherent in role.

10:30 a.m.   Break   (10)

10:40 a.m.   **The Priest in Catechetical Ministry** (continued)

- Analysis
    - Individual silent reflection/drawing during   (20)
      which each person draws a pie chart showing:
        - Breakdown of all activities   *[Handout 3]*
        - Focus on catechesis   *[Handout 4]*
    - Table discussion about reality illustrated by pie charts.   (10)
    - Revolving fishbowl   (90)
      (Empty chairs are placed in a circle in the center
      of the room—one for each table plus two additional
      chairs. To contribute to the discussion, a person
      must sit in one of the chairs. Once the person leaves,
      another person can join the circle to speak.)
        - What pattern did I/we see?
        - What concretely are priests doing in catechetical ministry?

Preparation for evening session: (10)
"How are you empowering catechists?"

- Participants review their responses in the reflection booklet before the evening session.

Assignment: *[Handout 5]*
The participants are asked to list the five most important things they do
in catechetical ministry as a priest. The lists are collected before lunch.   (10)

The Symposium Process

                                                                                  Approximate
                                                                                Time Allocation

DAY THREE (continued)

1:00 p.m.   Lunch

                    (Afternoon free)

5:15 p.m.   Hospitality

6:00 p.m.   Dinner

7:00 p.m.   **The Priest as Empowerer of Catechetical Ministry**

                    Roleplays   (60)

- Pastor and newly ordained Associate Pastor   *[Handouts 6, 7]*
  Issue: associate to be responsible for catechetical program

- Pastor and DRE   *[Handouts 8, 9]*
  Issue: sacramental preparation and lack of family involvement

- Pastor and Volunteer Catechist   *[Handouts 10, 11]*
  Issue: recruiting lay person to be volunteer catechist

[Key Issue: How *does* pastor *demonstrate* empowerment?]
- Discussion of issues after each role play.

8:00 p.m.   Action Research   (10)

- What do you do catechetically with . . . ?
  (A facilitator asks a series of questions and allows
  approximately 30 seconds for the participants to write
  a response to each. The responses are summarized and
  then distributed the following morning.)   *[Handout 12]*

8:10 p.m.   Brief Break   (05)

8:15 p.m.   **What Made Me the Priest I Am Today?**   (60)

- Individual reflection on the question:
  "What has or have been the most significant factors
  or influences that made you the priest you are today?"
- Sharing at each table
- Table report to group
- Discussion

                    Homework: *[Handout 13]*
As a result of what you've learned/ discussed,
what would you say to:
- Catechists
- Catechetical Leaders
- Priests
- Bishops

9:15 p.m.   Closing Prayer

9:30 p.m.   Hospitality

Approximate
Time Allocation

DAY FOUR

8:00	a.m.	Breakfast	
8:45	a.m.	**Opening Prayer**	(05)
8:50	a.m.	**The Priest as Empowerer of Catechetical Ministry** (continued)	(65)

- Review summaries of Action Research questions
- Homework (See Day Three evening)
    - Table discussion and summary
    - Table spokesperson reports to group
    - General discussion

9:55	a.m.	Brief Break	(05)
10:00	a.m.	**Exercise**: The participants write responses to the following questions. These responses are collected.	(15)

- What has this experience meant to you personally?
- What does this experience mean for your ministry?
- I now see that I empower catechetical ministry most effectively by . . .

10:15	a.m.	**General Discussion**	(30)
10:45	a.m.	**Conclusion**	(15)

- Expression of Thanks

11:00	a.m.	**Eucharist**
12:00	noon	Lunch and Departure

The Symposium Process

Handouts Used During the Symposium

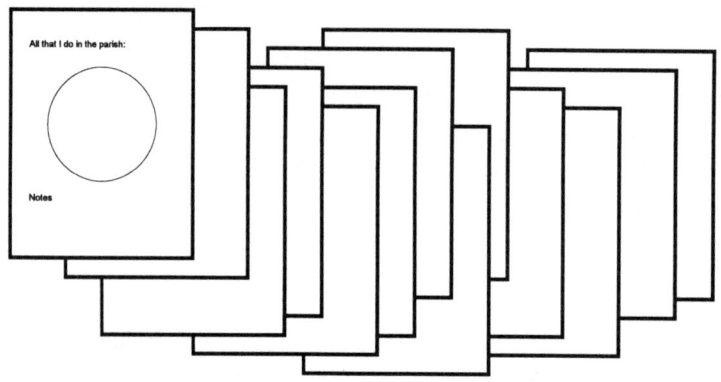

1. **Statement of Purpose**
   page 177

2. **Brief Agenda**
   page 178

3. **Parish Activities Chart**
   Chapter 3, page 76

4. **Catechetical Activities Chart**
   Chapter 3, page 77

5. **Five Most Important Catechetical Activities**
   Chapter 3, page 83

6. **Roleplay 1, Associate Pastor**
   Chapter 4, page 105

7. **Roleplay 1, Pastor**
   Chapter 4, page 106

8. **Roleplay 2, DRE**
   Chapter 4, page 111

9. **Roleplay 2, Pastor**
   Chapter 4, page 112

10. **Roleplay 3, Parishioner**
    Chapter 4, page 119

11. **Roleplay 3, Pastor**
    Chapter 4, page 120

12. **What do you do catechetically with . . .**
    Chapter 4, page 127

13. **As a result of the symposium process . . .**
    Chapter 5, page 136

Each participant at the symposium received this Statement of Purpose. You may want to provide a similar explanation to those attending a gathering modeled after the symposium.

STATEMENT OF PURPOSE

The **National Conference of Catechetical Leadership (NCCL)** and **William H. Sadlier, Inc.** are extremely pleased to sponsor this symposium, "The Priest as Empowerer of the Catechist."

This Symposium is a working conference in which all the participants will be invited to draw from their experience and expertise as they exchange ideas, dialogue, reflect, and develop plans that priests throughout the nation can use as they work to empower catechists.

The objectives, briefly stated, are:

- To identify elements needed for parish priests to empower those who serve in catechetical ministry;
- To identify concrete ways of helping and supporting parish priests in their empowering ministry.

The wisdom of each participant will help ensure an effective examination of this important topic. With the help of the Spirit, this event will stimulate and disseminate ideas for all who work to empower those in the ministry of catechesis.

The Symposium has been planned to enable the greatest participation of all assembled. To assist in achieving this goal NCCL President, Jim DeBoy, and Sadlier Vice President and Publisher, Jerry Baumbach, will serve as the Symposium's facilitators.

The symposium participants received an agenda such as this one.

AGENDA

DAY ONE

Arrival, Informal Gathering, and Recreation

DAY TWO

8:00	a.m.	Breakfast
8:45	a.m.	Opening of Symposium
9:30	a.m.	Opening Prayer
10:00	a.m.	Impact of the Parish
1:00	p.m.	Lunch

(Afternoon free)

5:15	p.m.	Hospitality
6:00	p.m.	Dinner
7:00	p.m.	Catechesis in the Parish
9:15	p.m.	Closing Prayer
9:30	p.m.	Hospitality

DAY THREE

8:00	a.m.	Breakfast
8:45	a.m.	Morning Prayer
9:00	a.m.	The Priest in Catechetical Ministry
1:00	p.m.	Lunch

(Afternoon free)

5:15	p.m.	Hospitality
6:00	p.m.	Dinner
7:00	p.m.	The Priest as Empowerer of Catechetical Ministry
9:15	p.m.	Closing Prayer
9:30	p.m.	Hospitality

DAY FOUR

8:00	a.m.	Breakfast
8:45	a.m.	Opening Prayer
8:50	a.m.	The Priest as Empowerer of Catechetical Ministry
10:00	a.m.	General Discussion
10:45	a.m.	Conclusion
11:00	a.m.	Eucharist
12:00	noon	Lunch and Departure

Appendix 1
Symposium Participants

Participants	Dioceses
Rev. Ralph L. Besendorfer	St. Augustine, FL
Rev. C. Paul Boudreau	Norwich, CT
Rev. Faustino Cruz, SM	Phoenix, AZ
Rev. Daniel J. Derry	San Jose, CA
Rev. Paul M. Dudziak	Washington, DC
Rev. Robert J. Farrell	Cincinnati, OH
Rev. Francis J. Flynn	Ogdensburg, NY
Rev. Charles A. Heidt	Bismarck, ND
Rev. David D. Kasperek	Green Bay, WI
Rev. Richard A. Kieran	Atlanta, GA
Rev. Joseph Lapauw, CICM	Brownsville, TX
Rev. Frank McCormick	Helena, MT
Rev. Kevin Minder	Yakima, WA
Rev. Jerome L. Morgan	Salina, KS
Rev. Paul M. Mullen	Scranton, PA
Rev. Terry M. Odien	Camden, NJ
Rev. Martin A. Peter	Indianapolis, IN
Rev. Joseph P. Plunkett	Newark, NJ
Rev. Henry S. Shelton	Jackson, MS
Rev. Thomas Sheridan	Cheyenne, WY
Rev. David A. Sork	Los Angeles, CA
Rev. Wilmer L. Todd	Houma-Thibodaux, LA
Rev. John Zeyack	Passaic, NJ (Byzantine)

Facilitators
Dr. Gerard F. Baumbach
James J. DeBoy, Jr.

National Conference of Catechetical Leadership
Mary Lou Barba, MCDP
Rev. Terry M. Odien
Neil A. Parent
James E. Tucker

National Catholic Educational Association
Robert Colbert

William H. Sadlier, Inc.
Dr. Eleanor Ann Brownell
Frank Sadlier Dinger
William Sadlier Dinger
Helen Hemmer, IHM
Karen Ryan

Appendix 2
Documents in this Book

Ad Gentes Divinitus, Decree on the Church's Missionary Activity December 7, 1965
Document of the Second Vatican Council

Adult Catechesis in the Christian Community 1990
This document reports the results of the sixth plenary session of the International Council for Catechesis. It focuses on and promotes the importance of adult catechesis in the faith community.

Apostolicam Actuositatem, Decree on the Apostolate of Lay People November 18, 1965
Document of the Second Vatican Council

Basic Teachings for Catholic Religious Education 1973
Prepared by the National Conference of Catholic Bishops in consultation with the Holy See, this document contains doctrinal principles to guide the faith formation of Catholic people.

Catechesi Tradendae, On Catechesis in Our Time 1979
This apostolic exhortation of Pope John Paul II on catechesis for today is especially significant for identifying the aim and purpose of catechesis.

Catechism of the Catholic Church 1994
This is a major catechism and reference resource for bishops, priests, catechetical leaders, publishers of catechetical material, and Catholic people.

The Challenge of Adolescent Catechesis 1986
This addresses the foundations and ministry of adolescent catechesis, indicates a framework for such catechesis, and incorporates leadership dimensions.

Christifideles Laici, Apostolic Exhortation on the Laity 1989
Pope John Paul II based his apostolic exhortation on the 1987 World Synod of Bishops who examined vocation and mission in the world 20 years after the Second Vatican Council.

Christus Dominus, Decree on the Pastoral Office of Bishops in the Church 1965
Document of the Second Vatican Council

Code of Canon Law 1983
The code contains the laws that govern the Church.

Dei Verbum, Dogmatic Constitution on Divine Revelation November 18, 1965
Document of the Second Vatican Council

Directory for the Life and Ministry of Priests 1994
This document, developed by the Congregation for the Clergy, addresses questions of a doctrinal and pastoral nature placed upon priests by the demands of evangelization.

Evangelii Nuntiandi, On Evangelization in the Modern World 1975
This apostolic exhortation of Pope Paul VI was a turning point in the Church's understanding of the relationship between culture and the faith message.

Documents in this Book

Familiaris Consortio, On the Family 1981
　The apostolic exhortation of Pope John Paul II builds upon the results of the Synod of Bishops. It addresses the value of marriage and the family, the role these play in society, as well as the pastoral care that marriage and family require.

A Family Perspective in Church and Society 1988
　Prepared by the bishops' Ad Hoc Committee on Marriage and Family Life, this document urges the Church and its leaders to incorporate a family perspective in all its policies, ministries and services, and it proposes ways of implementation.

Gaudium et Spes, Pastoral Constitution on the Church in the Modern World December 7, 1965
　Document of the Second Vatican Council

General Catechetical Directory 1971
　The Second Vatican Council called for a renewal of catechesis. In response, the *General Catechetical Directory,* prepared by the Sacred Congregation for the Clergy, presents guidelines for catechesis in the Church.

Go and Make Disciples 1993
　Drafted by the Bishops' Committee on Evangelization, this national plan and strategy for Catholic evangelization in the United States was approved and authorized by the National Conference of Catholic Bishops.

Gravissimum Educationis, Declaration on Christian Education October 28, 1965
　Document of the Second Vatican Council

Lumen Gentium, Dogmatic Constitution on the Church November 21, 1964
　Document of the Second Vatican Council

A Message to the People of God 1986
　This document reports the consensus of the Extraordinary Synod of Bishops who were called together by Pope John Paul II to reflect on the Second Vatican Council and its place in the life of the Church today.

Presbyterorum Ordinis, Decree on the Ministry and Life of Priests December 7, 1965
　Document of the Second Vatican Council

The Religious Dimension of Education in a Catholic School 1988
　Prepared by the Congregation for Catholic Education, this provides general guidelines for faith formation in Catholic Schools.

The Rite of Christian Initiation of Adults 1988
　Restored the catechumenate for initiation into the Church, with important implications for the entire process of conversion, liturgy, catechesis, and the faith community.

Sharing the Light of Faith: National Catechetical Directory for Catholics of the United States 1979
　Prepared by the National Conference of Catholic Bishops, this is a key resource for catechesis on all levels and the many dimensions of catechetical ministry. It contains a description of and guidelines for catechesis and catechetical planning in the United States.

To Teach as Jesus Did 1973
　A pastoral message on Catholic education that promotes message, community, and service as three critical elements for Catholic education.

Appendix 3
Selected Bibliography

Ad Hoc Committee on Marriage and Family Life, National Conference of Catholic Bishops. *A Family Perspective in Church and Society.* Washington, DC: USCC, 1988.

Baumbach, Gerard F. "Catechetical Roles: The DRE, the Priest, and the Catechist." *Catechist Magazine* (September 1980): 54-56.

Baumbach, Gerard F., and James J. DeBoy, Jr. "Symposium Examines Priests' Empowering Role in Catechesis." *Caravan* Volume 8, Number 30 (Spring 1994): 4-5.

Baumbach, Gerard F. "Symposium Examines Catechetical Empowerment by Parish Priests." *Momentum* Volume XXV, Number 1 (February/March 1994): 64-65.

Bishops' Committee on the Parish. *The Parish: A People, a Mission, a Structure.* Washington, DC: USCC, 1981.

Bishops' Committee on Priestly Life and Ministry. *The Continuing Formation of Priests: Growing in Wisdom, Age and Grace.* Washington, DC: USCC, 1985.

Bishops' Committee on Priestly Life and Ministry. *A Shepherd's Care: Reflections on the Changing Role of Pastor.* Washington, DC: USCC, 1987.

Bishops of New Jersey. "Catechetical Ministry Attuned to the Signs of the Times, Pastoral Letter to Religious Educators." *Origins* 22 (October 8, 1992): 289-298.

Bishops of New York State. *Journeying Toward a Future Full of Promise: Catechesis in New York State, Reflections and Challenges.* Albany: NY State Catholic Conference, 1988.

Brown, Kathy, and Frank C. Sokol, eds. *Issues in the Christian Initiation of Children: Catechesis and Liturgy.* Chicago: Liturgy Training Publications, 1989.

Burns, John. *Affirming the Catechist.* Washington, DC: NCDD, undated.

Byers, David, ed. *The Parish in Transition.* Washington, DC: USCC, 1986.

Canon Law Society of America. *Code of Canon Law, Latin–English Edition.* Washington, DC: Canon Law Society of America, 1983.

Catechism of the Catholic Church for the United States of America. Washington DC: United States Catholic Conference, Inc.—Libreria Editrice Vaticana, 1994.

Chicago Studies. (Issue addresses the *Catechism of the Catholic Church*). *Chicago Studies* Volume 33 (April 1994): 1-93..

The Congregation for Catholic Education. *The Religious Dimension of Education in a Catholic School.* Washington, DC: USCC, 1988.

Congregation for the Clergy. *Directory for the Life and Ministry of Priests.* Washington, DC: USCC, 1994.

Congregation for the Evangelization of Peoples. *Guide for Catechists.* Washington, DC: USCC, 1993.

Coriden, James A., Thomas J. Green, and Donald E. Heintschel, eds. *The Code of Canon Law: A Text and Commentary.* New York: Paulist Press, 1985.

Dalglish, William A. *Models for Catechetical Ministry in the Rural Parish.* Washington, DC: NCDD, 1981.

Selected Bibliography

DeBoy, James J., Jr. *Getting Started in Adult Religious Education: A Practical Guide.* New York: Paulist Press, 1979.

Dolan, Jay P., R. Scott Appleby, Patricia Byrne, and Debra Campbell. *Transforming Parish Ministry: The Changing Roles of Catholic Clergy, Laity, and Women Religious.* New York: Crossroad, 1990.

Downs, Thomas. *The Parish as Learning Community: Modeling for Parish and Adult Growth.* New York: Paulist Press, 1979.

Duggan, Robert D. *The Order of Christian Initiation of Adults and the Future of Catechetics.* Washington, DC: NCDD, 1990.

Evangelization in the Culture and Society of the United States and the Bishop as Teacher of the Faith: Meeting of His Holiness John Paul II with the Archbishops of the United States. Washington, DC: USCC, 1989.

Extraordinary Synod of Bishops. *A Message to the People of God* and *The Final Report.* Washington, DC: USCC, 1986.

Flannery, O.P., Austin, gen. ed. *Vatican Council II: The Conciliar and Post Conciliar Documents.* Northport, NY: Costello Publishing Company, 1992.
- *The Constitution on the Sacred Liturgy (Sacrosanctum concilium)*, December 4, 1963
- *Dogmatic Constitution on the Church (Lumen Gentium)*, November 21, 1964
- *Declaration on Christian Education (Gravissimum educationis)*, October 28, 1965
- *Decree on the Pastoral Office of Bishops in the Church (Christus Dominus)*, October 28, 1965
- *Dogmatic Constitution on Divine Revelation (Dei verbum)*, November 18, 1965
- *Decree on the Apostolate of Lay People (Apostolicam actuositatem)*, November 18, 1965
- *Decree on the Church's Missionary Activity (Ad gentes divinitus)*, December 7, 1965
- *Pastoral Constitution on the Church in the Modern World (Gaudium et spes)*, December 7, 1965
- *Decree on the Ministry and Life of Priests (Presbyterorum Ordinis)*, December 7, 1965

Friend, William B., Elinor R. Ford, and Margaret Daues. *Evangelizing the Cultures in A.D. 2000.* Copyright by Diocese of Shreveport. New York: William H. Sadlier, Inc., 1990.

Groome, Thomas H. *Christian Religious Education, Sharing Our Story and Vision.* San Francisco: Harper San Francisco, 1980.

Groome, Thomas H. *Sharing Faith: A Comprehensive Approach to Religious Education and Pastoral Ministry, The Way of Shared Praxis.* San Francisco: Harper San Francisco, 1991.

Hater, Robert J. *New Visions, New Directions: Implementing the Catechism of the Catholic Church.* Chicago: Thomas More, 1994.

Hater, Robert J. *Parish Catechetical Ministry.* Mission Hills, CA: Benziger, 1986.

Hater, Robert J. *The Relationship Between Evangelization and Catechesis.* Washington, DC: NCDD, 1982.

Hater, Robert J. *Religious Education and Catechesis: A Shift in Focus.* Washington, DC: NCDD, 1982.

Hater, Robert J. *The Role of a Diocesan Religious Education/Catechetical Office.* Washington, DC: NCDD, 1982.

Herrera, Marina. *Adult Religious Education for the Hispanic Community.* Washington, DC: NCDD undated.

Hofinger, Johannes. "Looking Backward and Forward: Journey of Catechesis." *The Living Light* 2 (June 1984): 348-357.

Hughes, Jane W., ed. *Ministering to Adult Learners.* Washington, DC: USCC, 1981.

International Council for Catechesis. *Adult Catechesis in the Christian Community: Some Principles and Guidelines.* Washington, DC: USCC, 1992.

Ivory, Thomas P. *Conversion and Community: A Catechumenal Model for Total Parish Formation.* New York: Paulist Press, 1988.

Jewitt, Bernard C. *The Role of the Parish Priest in Catechetical Ministry.* Washington, DC: NCDD, 1977.

Kelly, Francis D., Peter L. Benson and Michael J. Donahue. *Toward Effective Parish Religious Education for Children and Young People: A National Study.* Washington, DC: NCEA, 1986.

Mongoven, Anne Marie. "Catechetics in the 90's: Present State and Future Challenges." *Chicago Studies* 31 (November 1992): 229-243.

Mongoven, Anne Marie. *Signs of Catechesis: An Overview of the National Catechetical Directory.* New York: Paulist Press, 1979.

National Catholic Educational Association. *Collaborators in Catechesis: Bishops, Publishers, Diocesan Directors.* Washington, DC: NCEA, 1990.

National Conference of Catholic Bishops. *Basic Teachings for Catholic Religious Education.* Washington, DC: USCC, 1973.

National Conference of Catholic Bishops. *The Challenge of Peace: God's Promise and Our Response.* Washington, DC: USCC, 1983.

National Conference of Catholic Bishops. *Economic Justice for All: Pastoral Letter on Catholic Social Teaching and the U.S. Economy.* Washington, DC: USCC, 1986.

National Conference of Catholic Bishops. *Go and Make Disciples: A National Plan and Strategy for Catholic Evangelization in the United States.* Washington, DC: USCC, 1993.

National Conference of Catholic Bishops. *Guidelines for Doctrinally Sound Catechetical Materials.* Washington, DC: USCC, 1990.

National Conference of Catholic Bishops. *A Manual for Bishops: Rights and Responsibilities of Diocesan Bishops in the Revised Code of Canon Law, Revised Edition.* Washington, DC: USCC, 1992.

National Conference of Catholic Bishops. *Program of Priestly Formation.* Washington, DC: USCC, 1993.

National Conference of Catholic Bishops. *Sharing the Light of Faith: National Catechetical Directory for Catholics of the United States.* Washington, DC: USCC, 1979.

National Conference of Catholic Bishops. *To Teach as Jesus Did.* Washington, DC: USCC, 1973.

National Conference of Catholic Bishops. *The Teaching Ministry of the Diocesan Bishop.* Washington, DC: USCC, 1992.

Selected Bibliography

National Conference of Diocesan Directors. *Priestly Formation and Catechetics: Resources for Seminary Formation for the Catechetical Ministry.* Washington, DC: NCCD, 1986.

National Federation for Catholic Youth Ministry. *The Challenge of Adolescent Catechesis: Maturing in Faith.* 1986.

O'Brien, J. Stephen. *An Urgent Task: What Bishops and Priests Say About Religious Education Programs.* Washington, DC: NCEA, 1988.

Parent, Neil A. "The Priest as Empowerer of Catechetical Ministry." *Focus on Catechetical Leadership* Volume 5, Number 2 (March/April 1993): 1, 8-9.

Parent, Neil A., ed. *Agenda for the 90s: Forging the Future of Adult Religious Education.* Washington, DC: USCC, 1989.

Parent, Neil A., ed. *Christian Adulthood: A Catechetical Resource.* Washington, DC: USCC, (issued annually).

Parent, Neil A., ed. *Educating for Christian Maturity.* Washington, DC: USCC, 1990.

Pollard, John. "Catechesis: A Pastoral Priority." *The Living Light* 28 (Spring 1992): 199-209.

Pope John Paul II. *On the Permanent Validity of the Church's Missionary Mandate (Redemptoris Missio).* Washington, DC: USCC, 1990.

Pope John Paul II. *On Catechesis in Our Time (Catechesi Tradendae).* Washington, DC: USCC, 1979.

Pope John Paul II. *On the Family (Familiaris Consortio).* Washington, DC: USCC, 1981.

Pope John Paul II. *The Vocation and the Mission of the Lay Faithful in the Church and in the World, (Christifideles Laici).* Washington, DC: USCC, 1988.

Pope Paul VI. *On Evangelization in the Modern World (Evangelii Nuntiandi).* Washington, DC: USCC, 1975.

Purcell, OSB, Antoinette, and Rev. Martin Weithman. *Developing a Parish Plan for Family Catechesis.* Washington, DC: NCCL, 1994.

Reichert, Richard. "Catechists Confront Ecclesiological Schizophrenia." *The Living Light* 28 (Winter 1992): 166-174.

Rite of Christian Initiation of Adults (Study Edition). Washington, DC: USCC, 1988.

Sacred Congregation for the Clergy. *General Catechetical Directory.* Washington, DC: USCC, 1971.

Schwartz, Robert M. *Servant Leaders of the People of God: An Ecclesial Spirituality for American Priests.* New York: Paulist Press, 1989.

Sinwell, Joseph P., and Billie Poon, eds. *The Future of Ministry: The New England Symposium Papers.* New York: William H. Sadlier, Inc., 1985.

Sinwell, Joseph P., and Karen H. Hinman, eds. *Breaking Open the Word of God: Resources for Using the Lectionary for Catechesis in the RCIA (Cycle A).* New York: Paulist Press, 1986.

Sinwell, Joseph P., and Karen H. Hinman, eds. *Breaking Open the Word of God: Resources for Using the Lectionary for Catechesis in the RCIA (Cycle B).* New York: Paulist Press, 1987.

Sinwell, Joseph P., Thomas P. Walters, and Rita T. Walters. *National Profile of Diocesan Directors of Religious Education.* Washington, DC: NCEA.

Study of the Studies Task Force. *A Report on the State of Catechesis in the United States.* Washington, DC: USCC, 1990.

Sweetser, Thomas P. "Fostering Spiritual Growth Through Parish Structures." *New Theology Review* 5 (November 1992): 5-21.

Synod of Bishops. *Instrumentum Laboris: The Formation of Priests in Circumstances of the Present Day.* Rome, 1990.

United States Conference of Catholic Bishops. *Putting Children and Families First, A Challenge for Our Church, Nation, and World.* Washington, DC: USCC 1991.

Walters, Thomas P. *DRE: Issues and Concerns for the 80's.* Washington, DC: NCDD, 1983.

Walters, Thomas P, and Arthur J. Kubick. *DRE Yesterday, Today, and Tomorrow.* Washington, DC: NCEA/NCDD, 1990.

Wilde, James A. *Before and After Baptism: The Work of Teachers and Catechists.* Chicago: Liturgy Training Publications, 1988.

Wilde, James A. *Parish Catechumenate: Pastors, Presiders, Preachers.* Chicago: Liturgy Training Publications, 1988.

Acknowledgments

Scripture selections are taken from the *New American Bible* Copyright © 1991, 1986, 1970 by the Confraternity of Christian Doctrine, Washington, DC and are used with permission. All rights reserved.

Selections from: *Sharing the Light of Faith: National Catechetical Directory for Catholics of the United States* Copyright © 1979 United States Catholic Conference (USCC), Washington, DC; *Go and Make Disciples: A National Plan and Strategy for Catholic Evangelization in the United States* © 1993 USCC; *Basic Teachings for Catholic Religious Education*, © 1973 USCC; *A Family Perspective in Church and Society* © 1988 USCC; *General Catechetical Directory* © 1971 USCC; *A Message to the People of God and The Final Report* © 1986 USCC; *To Teach as Jesus Did* © 1973 USCC; *Adult Catechesis in the Christian Community: Some Principles and Guidelines – With Discussion Guide* © 1992 USCC; *Catechism of the Catholic Church* for the United States of America © 1994 USCC-Libreria Editrice Vaticana are used with permission. All rights reserved.

Excerpts from *Vatican Council II: The Conciliar and Post Conciliar Documents, New Revised Edition*, edited by Austin Flannery, OP, copyright © 1992, Costello Publishing Company, Inc., Northport, NY are used by permission of the publisher, all rights reserved. No part of these excerpts may be reproduced, stored in a retrieval system, or transmitted in any form or by any means—electronic, mechanical, photocopying, recording or otherwise, without express permission of Costello Publishing Company.

Excerpts from *The Challenge of Adolescent Catechesis: Maturing in Faith*, Copyright © 1986 The National Federation for Catholic Youth Ministry, Inc., 3700-A Oakview Terrace, N.E., Washington, DC 20017-2591. All rights reserved. Used with permission.

Excerpts from the *Code of Canon Law, Latin/English Edition*, are used with permission, copyright © 1983 Canon Law Society of America, Washington, DC.

Text from the *Rite of Christian Initiation of Adults* © 1985, International Committee on English in the Liturgy, Inc. (ICEL). All rights reserved.

Rev. Msgr. James T. Mahoney was unable to attend the symposium, but completed and submitted the reflection questions. We are grateful for his responses, some of which have been incorporated into this book.

Cover Design
Ana Jouvin

Cover Illustrator
Andrew Muonio